THE NEW MIDDLE AGES

THE NEW MIDDLE AGES

WOMEN IN MIDLIFE

JEAN MARMOREO MD

Prentice
Hall
Canada

A Pearson Company
Toronto

Canadian Cataloguing in Publication Data

Marmoreo, Jean
    The new middle ages : women in midlife

Includes index.

ISBN 0-13-066383-2

1. Middle ages women—Health and hygiene. I. Title.

RA778.M37 2002   613'.04244   C2001-903675-2

ISBN 0-13-066383-2

Editorial Director, Trade Division: Andrea Crozier
Acquisitions Editor: Andrea Crozier
Managing Editor: Tracy Bordian
Copy Editor: Judy Phillips
Proofreader: Kat Mototsune
Art Direction: Mary Opper
Cover Design: Julia Hall
Cover Image: Photonica
Interior Design: Julia Hall
Production Manager: Kathrine Pummell
Page Layout: B.J. Weckerle

 2 3 4 5 WEB   06 05 04 03 02

Printed and bound in Canada.

This publication contains the opinions and ideas of its author and is designed to provide useful advice in regard to the subject matter covered. The herbs and other treatments in this book are described for the information and education of readers. They are not a replacement for diagnosis and treatment by qualified health professionals. The author and publisher are not engaged in rendering health or other professional services in this publication. This publication is not intended to provide a basis for action in particular circumstances without consideration by a competent professional. The author and publisher expressly disclaim any responsibility for any liability, loss, or risk, personal or otherwise, which is incurred as a consequence, directly or indirectly, of the use and application of any of the contents of this book.

ATTENTION: CORPORATIONS
Books are available at quantity discounts with bulk purchase for educational, business, or sales promotional use. For information, please email or write to: Pearson PTR Canada, Special Sales, PTR Division, 26 Prince Andrew Place, Don Mills, Ontario, M3C 2T8. Email **ss.corp@pearsoned.com**. Please supply: title of book, ISBN, quantity, how the book will be used, date needed.

Visit the Prentice Hall Canada Web site! Send us your comments, browse our catalogues, and more. **www.pearsonptr.ca**

A Pearson Company

To my patients
whose lives became stories
to guide other women's lives

CONTENTS

Acknowledgments

This book grew out of my columns for the *National Post*, which found an audience largely because no one was writing about the real issues that concern one of the largest, fastest-growing, yet most invisible audiences anywhere: midlife women.

But the idea for having a column in the first place was motivated more by serendipity than anything else. My husband said one night over dinner, "You should write a column about middle-aged women." Then our friend Helga Stephenson said: "Let me talk to the people at the *National Post*." Then another friend, Ron Moore, said: "You should call the column *The Middle Ages*." And so it came to pass. A thousand words every two weeks on the issues that bedevil and cheer women in the middle of their lives.

It soon became clear that what the newspaper's readers wanted was stories, suitably anonymous, of women like themselves, who had faced challenges like their own. These are the stories I chose to tell, and they form the basis of this book. These stories are concise and human largely because of the encouragement and superb editing by Dianne de Fenoyl and her associate Sheilagh McEvenue of the *National Post*. I also want to thank Dianne for carrying the torch for the column and seeing it safely ensconced with the *Saturday Post*, after a round of cutbacks last fall at the newspaper.

Morphing the columns into a book was not serendipity at all; indeed, it was largely through the efforts of my agent, Michael Levine, that Prentice Hall Canada agreed to tackle in book form the audience that the *National Post* has reached out to in the columns.

For what is in your hands right now, I have Andrea Crozier to thank. As the Editorial Director of Prentice Hall Canada, she saw that there was something larger than a newspaper column in the stories that my patients bring to the examining room, and encouraged the "physician voice" in the book.

I owe an inestimable thanks to my friend and editor, Paula Chabanais. Her commitment to completing this book was total, something that would waver in most people, when the writer is a doctor with a full-time practice. Paula has educated me in the ways of writing, publishing, and editing that does full justice to her more than two decades as one of Canada's leading authors' midwives.

And finally, I want to thank my family: My three children who are always there to remind me, as with all of us, what life is all about. And with great love, there is my debt to my husband and first editor, Bob Ramsay, my soul mate and late-life treasure.

Introduction:
How It All Began

Being a woman is hard work. Not without joy and even ecstasy, but still relentless unending work. Becoming an old female may require only being born with certain genitalia, inheriting long living genes and the fortune not to be run over by an out-of-control truck, but to become and remain a woman commands the existence and employment of genius.

Maya Angelou

The start was seemingly innocuous. An article for a new newspaper column called "The Middle Ages" about middle-aged women, women I had looked after as patients for a generation. Growing with them, reveling in their accomplishments, triumphs of marriage, motherhood, school success, work. Seeing them through the tough times, comforting, advocating, defending, holding—yes, holding too—and sometimes even crying with them. The article was also an acknowledgment of the difficulties of being a middle-aged woman in today's youth-based culture, of being invisible. Of being, at the same time and of necessity, a care provider in two directions— to parents and to children; of having responsibility for home and career; of juggling the world out there and the hearth and home; and of striving to have it all—great job; admiring friends; talented, bright, and respectful children; a considerate lover in an outstanding spouse. Oh, and of making time for self-improvement and personal growth, giving back to the community and being a world citizen, caring for the environment, and rallying for social justice and animal rights. And looking good!

Any family physician who has practiced for 20 years, as I have, begins to see the patterns in people's lives and the discrepancies in how society treats a particular kind of patient. Most of my 2,000 patients are women, and many of them have progressed from having babies to having menopause. I have joined them in this journey and, at 59 years of age, I count myself among those Canadian women who are middle aged.

Being a middle-aged woman in Canada today means many things. But most of all, it means being largely invisible—to marketers, legislators, and lovers. And yet, there are 3 million women in Canada today between the ages of 40 and 65. Despite the tidal wave of Gen-Xers we gave birth to, it is we who make up the fastest growing segment of Canadian society. Five years from now, middle-aged women will make up some 20 percent of this country's population and, given the steady influx of women to positions of influence, a significant percentage of our nation's wealth will rest in their hands.

I do not begrudge society's tendency to marginalize middle-aged women. I know it is mainly a function of how youth and beauty continue to rule everything from purchasing decisions to systemic discriminations. Actually, many of my patients say it is a relief not to have to worry about that stuff anmore. It's a relief to have the kids grown up and gone, because these middle-aged women can now start doing what they want to do, rather than what they've had to do. For some it's changing their career, leaving their husbands, taking a lover, or buying a muscle car.

Yet largely because society has forgotten about middle-aged women, I have found middle-aged women are generally unprepared for this most important part of their life's journey, which can be confusing and frightening. Many women arrive in my office panic-stricken at the prospect of being unemployed

> *One is not born a woman; one becomes one.*
>
> *—Simone de Beauvoir,* The Second Sex

now that they've been caught in downsizing and outsourcing and have to find a new livelihood, because each believes, at her core, that her family would soon be visiting the food bank if it didn't have at least two incomes. Or their children are grown up and *not* gone. Or their husband has left for a younger woman, or just up and died (in Canada, men die on average six years earlier than women).

Others are so frantically busy, they are panic-stricken with fear of not being able to keep all the balls from crashing to earth. Some of them have high-powered jobs that gobble up 12 hours of every day. For them, the answer is to seriously reexamine their lives and priorities, though most will resist doing so, at least initially.

Very few of these women come into my examining room and say: "I'm burning out. I've got to get out." Rather, they begin by saying: "I can't understand why I'm always so tired." Or: "Our kids are acting out and my husband can't control them." Or: "I got up to leave after making a two-hour presentation to the senior management committee, and I couldn't move, my back was in such spasm."

But when I gently suggest that I sign their short-term disability papers, many of them view this logical and reasonable solution as the ultimate defeat. Their dismay, often not verbalized or even recognized at first, turns to shock when I next say that 6 to 12 weeks is the time they should think of taking off in order to get well.

"But what will I do with all that time?" are usually their first words. Yet—and this is even more telling—very often, at the end of such a hiatus, we are just beginning to see the problem, and no solution seems in sight.

Many of my patients also face the task of taking care of their aging and frail parents. Financially stretched and strapped for time (and often living hundreds of miles away), they dread the prospect of being their parents' advocate in our health care system, let alone engaging in that exquisitely painful dance that precedes placing them in a retirement home. But they also dread not doing these things.

Some of the chapters in this book are designed to provide a "short appointment" format for the busy woman and so answer the questions that are most often asked in the setting of the doctor's office. These chapters are in my voice, that of a physician caring for midlife women. They also tell of the experience of some of my patients, and of the strength and determination of these women. It is my hope that women will be able to find information that is useful or interesting to them or that has particular relevance. This book is meant to be dipped into—scanned for information or example as the need or interest arises.

While writing the chapter on breasts, and specifically about the issues concerning breast cancer, it became clear to me that the very best information I can provide is information that will assist women in discovering the Internet resources and support groups that are now so prevalent and readily accessible. In the face of changing treatments and new results from clinical trials, websites are a vital tool and resource for those women who want information on evolving treatments and new insights.

Beyond medical or scientific data, the support of other women has always been a remarkable source of comfort and strength during the tough times of diagnosis and treatment. The prime purpose of this book is to give a voice to those women I am privileged to care for. By no means are all my patients driven careerists. The majority are struggling to make ends meet, to keep their families and themselves happy, and to avoid the thousand plagues their flesh is heir to. Their stories, told for the most part anonymously, are what I have brought to these pages. This is a book in their voices, reflecting their concerns and fears, their strengths and convictions, their efforts and their joy. It is a book about how women *do* manage to juggle all the balls or at least enough of them to keep on going through troubles and stresses and come out on the other side.

It is very much their stories and their feelings that will provide the context of a meaningful encounter that comes from reading about what you know in your heart. Whether it is caring for parents on the one side and teenagers on the other; whether it is balancing the experience of downsizing with learning the new career skills you now require; whether it is leaving or replacing a lover or starting a whole new existence; whether it is gearing up to do battle with illness or to settle into pleasure and reward, this is a book for all women of an age and for their families.

I have preserved the anonymity of most of these women and their stories, though a number of times the six degrees of separation get me into trouble when identities are revealed by the fact that our city of 4 million is, after all, a small town. Some of these stories also required more interview time than my busy office schedule permitted, necessitating offsite interviews. As I finished one of these interviews, I realized that the children of my patient had meandered in and out of our view many more times than we had expected. "I had better reassure your boys that I've not been sitting out here in your backyard with you because you're sick," I said. Immediately, my patient stepped into the house and told her boys she wasn't ill, and that I was there because I was writing a book for women. They took the news with a nod, visibly relaxing, then chatted easily while mom did a very mom thing. She took a jar of canned tomatoes and gave it to me to take home.

I did seek Esther Meyer's permission to tell her story. She is too well known in the community of Canada's yoga teachers to preserve her anonymity while offering her strength as an example for other women. She kindly agreed both to the disclosure and to an in-depth interview, which permitted me to explore more deeply her remarkable story.

Judy Rebick, another of Canada's well-known "daughters," also kindly consented to the disclosure of identity as well as to the reversal of interviewer-interviewee roles. Her story is a definitive example of what I call the vision from the platform: the summation of all our talents and experiences pointing the way or dragging us into the future.

I hope that by writing this book I have given back one fraction of the inspiration that going to work every day gives me. My patients are a source of wonder and pride. Caring for them and their families is my privilege. Writing about them is a joy. They are truly beacons for our future.

I

MIDDLE AGE:
THE TIME CRUNCH

Half our life is spent trying to find something to do with the time we have rushed through life trying to save.

WILL ROGERS

Women often bemoan the fact that menopause takes so long. Menopause can last 10 years—from age 45 to age 55. Therefore, a good chunk of it takes place during middle age—that phase in a woman's life when she's considered to be neither there nor there. Not that middle age and menopause need be joined at the hip or even spoken of in the same breath. But they usually are, and there are many hand-in-glove links that make both the process of menopause and the state of being hang together.

The greatest of these links is one of time. Women just do not have time for menopause. But while *they* don't even have time for marking the start of the process, pharmaceutical companies, governmental planning sectors, and nongovernmental organizations with health initiatives can't wait for it to begin. And so it is that in most publications, age 50 defines menopause and hence influences most of our perceptions about it. The truth is that because no one knows when menopause starts or ends, since as an event it can be defined only by the prolonged absence of another event, menopause cannot be neatly wrapped and filed away.

Menopause can be both a blessing and a watershed for many midlife women, a time when they can come to terms with the life they have known and with the life they look forward to. Yet, as though the physiology of menopause, with its accompanying mood swings, irregular periods, and flushing, is not enough of a burden to shoulder, most women are already hard-pressed to accomplish all they need to do before they can even get to bed—never mind dealing with sleep disturbances. As much as menopause is a nuisance, it is rarely a life threat. In fact, most women sail through without any serious problems once there. However, the process does get muddied when added to all the other constraints that beset busy women. As the bulk of the baby boomers are now set to "go through" (in North America, they are turning 50 at the rate of one every 15 seconds), the issues around menopause are intricately woven with the issues around time and how it is used—a fact that explains the reaction to my first article about women in midlife being constantly tired. Clearly the message hit a chord. The response was instantaneous; women were banging on my door, and the phone rang off the hook. Part of the reason for such a response may have related to my suggested willingness to document stress-leave qualifications for my patients, but mostly it reflected an acknowledgment of what many women were voicing.

Time, like the sword of Damocles, hangs over a number of my patients. It feels ever present and unpleasant. The more they try to get out from under, the more they become trapped. Time management, time for yourself, time off, time-out, down time, quality time; we have come to live in bits and bytes of time and, universally, the lament is that there is not enough of it. This lack and dread is perhaps the greatest pressure that I see midlife women struggling with—trying to make time for everything they have to do.

> *Turning 50 at the rate of one every 15 seconds, the bulk of the baby boomers are now set to "go through."*

THE TIME-CRUNCH

The Time Study

In the mid-1990s, two professors, John Robinson and Geoffrey Godbey, undertook to publish the then definitive work about time and how Americans use it. Entitled *Time for Life: the Surprising Ways Americans Use Their Time*, the study was exhaustive and examined time usage across all ages, classes, and genders—comparing Americans with other indigenous cultural and racial groups and with other countries. The means of study was an elaborate and detailed time diary, a tool the authors took great pains to cross-compare with surveys, polls, and other measures to ensure the accuracy of their findings. The study compared the use of time over a 30-year span, from the 1960s to the 1990s. Remarkably, and across all ages, classes, and genders, the authors reported that Americans in the 1990s had a net gain of six hours per week of free time.

Six hours more each week—for every child, woman, man, retiree. More than they had enjoyed 30 years before. The next question Robinson and Godbey asked was, How was all this extra time being used? The finding?

Watching television, an activity that accounted for an average of 15 to 20 hours per week. And regardless of age, sex, ethnicity, and social position, there was a proportionate increase in each group. Even fitness and holidays, reading and conversation—all those activities we crave time to do—all those activities together did not show any significant increase when people had extra free time. Rather, these activities, which did show modest increases during the 30-year span, were dwarfed by the increased time spent in front of the television.

Now, none of this made sense to me. Most of my patients and I can count on one hand the hours spent (weekly) in front of the TV. If there is any free time to be gleaned, it most certainly will not be spent watching television. I went back over the study's charts and data, looking for an explanation. The authors were clear that since 1985, women, particularly working women, felt more rushed and had greater perceived stress than men. Perceived stress was highest amongst the middle-aged, peaking at age 44 and dropping dramatically after age 54.

Although there is no Canadian counterpart for the US study, Statistics Canada publishes a report on Canadian women every five years, the most recent being *Women in Canada 2000*. While many of its categories are different and the time span studied more recent, both publications discuss the topic of time stress.

Child Care and Shopping

Women continue to do 40 percent more of the shopping for the household than men, a figure virtually unchanged since 1965.

According to *Women in Canada 2000*, in 1998, 38 percent of Canadian women (ages 25 to 44) employed full time reported feeling severely time stressed. Indeed, both publications conclude that almost 80 percent of child care—particularly the custodial tasks, meal preparation, cleaning, and feeding—falls to women. What has changed between the 1960s and now is that there are fewer children, more of whom are being raised by single mothers.

In both the United States and Canada, women's share of unpaid work hours has remained consistently higher than men's. Two areas that show little change are child care and elder care (the US study did not include the latter category but did include shopping). The US diaries from 1985 showed that about 24 hours per week were spent in some form of housework, shopping, or child care, and that women spent about double the time in these activities than men. If a woman takes a job, the time allotted to family care decreases by about one-third. Nonetheless, the chores and child care that remain do not get delegated to the spouse; rather, they continue as a part of the expectations on a woman's time. It adds to her "time pressure" and "feeling rushed" quotient. In Canada in 1998, married women employed full time with at least one child under age 19 living at home averaged 4.9 hours per day on unpaid work activities—an hour and a half more than their male counterparts. No wonder women don't feel there is more free time.

In the US study, in the area of shopping (there are no statistics for shopping in Statistic Canada's breakdown of unpaid hours), women continue to do 40 percent more of the shopping for the household than men, a figure virtually unchanged since 1965. Women who are required to manage the family's household budget, purchase food and goods for the week, and make the lunches are hardly in a position to delegate the weekly shopping. I remember when my housekeeper, the person who managed the household for me because I had no time to do so, reported with a worried air that the week's grocery bill was consistently topping $120. Could I have done any better? Not at all, and would I have anyone else do it, as in my husband? No way.

> *There is scarcely any less bother in the running of a family than in that of an entire state. And domestic business no less importunate for being less important.*
>
> *—Michel de Montaigne, 1533–1592*

Women do not hang on to the shopping responsibility because they are inveterate shopaholics; they do so because they know what can be bought to get the job done quickly and with the least effort. This is not to say that men cannot do the shopping and, according to the US time study, many male retirees do assume this role. A fact, I would suggest, that reflects the increase in available time to cook and clean for a spouse who is at home or whose wife is ailing in a manner that requires this contribution from the man. We assume there is more sharing and more division of household tasks between house partners today, but the time study shows no and no, respectively, over a long period.

Who's Looking After the Elders?

While there was no data on elder care in the US study, Statistics Canada reports that in 1999, women constituted 69.8 percent of the 85-and-older age group, and 62 percent of them lived in private households. Within my practice, I know how much time is spent by my women patients taking their parents to appointments and managing their affairs. I can put numbers to those who have taken a leave of absence, a sabbatical, or just plain quit their jobs in order to look after frail relatives.

It may be that looking after parents wasn't much of an issue in the 1960s or '70s. It may be that the graying of America hasn't been seen as a time issue. Clearly, a study of time that omits elder care does not paint a complete picture, as the "too rushed" feeling most certainly applies to this swiftly increasing area of care needs.

Another omission in the US time study is the emerging issue of the sandwich generation, that is, those who are raising their children while also caring for aging parents. As with most other family care responsibilities, the fear is that these duties will fall disproportionately on women, thus further adding to the time-crunch of women. In fact, in 1996, almost one million Canadian women between the ages of 25 and 54—15 percent of all women in the age group—provided both unpaid child care and care or assistance to a senior, compared to only 9 percent of men in the same age group.

It's Not How Much You Have But What You Do with It

One of the remarkable issues to emerge from the US study was the effect of all the labor-saving devices now available to the busy homemaker. Surely these devices reduce the time required to do household chores, thereby increasing leisure time? Apparently not. The study showed that in spite of dishwashers, microwaves, and so on, the amount of time gained by not doing household chores did not change that much. And, for nonwork activities where efficiency wasn't the issue, people are prepared to spend any amount of time if that activity rewards them or is of their choosing.

> *Hatred of domestic work is a natural and admirable result of civilization.*
>
> —Rebecca West

One of life's gifts to many women as they age is the ability to make extraordinary shifts in how their time is spent. Like one of my patients who took a sabbatical from her teaching job and for one year became nanny for her daughter's child. "A wonderful year," she recalls. "Morning walks with the baby. Every day we would be out, talking to neighbors. Being out with a baby makes everyone happy to talk with you, especially if you're gray-haired. They assume you have more time, I think."

DELEGATING TIME

This chapter would not be complete without acknowledging that women must and do, with regularity, delegate responsibility to their mates, their children, their "sisters." How else would it all get done? But for busy women, it is often the why (because she needs to find a job, change careers, spend more time with her aging parents, and so on) that finally determines the how and the what. In other words, those things that are parceled out are not randomly selected. As with everything in the life of midlife women, there is still an efficiency quotient that needs to be met.

My patients seem to be engaged in the full-time business of what one of my patients calls "exquisite time management." At age 40, she decided she wanted to return to school after 10 years of working and mothering. Not just any schooling, but schooling that demands vast amounts of hands-on training—what we used to call an apprenticeship. She is required to attend class for 30 hours a week, then do a practicum for another 30, on top of tending to her two boys and husband. You might say that anyone who works 60 hours a week and runs a full-time household is, of course, going to feel stretched—and yes, husband and children have had to pitch in and help. My patient told me that one Sunday, as she sat at home studying anatomy in gruesome detail, she looked out on her husband who was doing all the yard-work, with their boys lending a hand. They were even trimming her rose of Sharon. "And believe me," she said, "he knows how I love them and no one trims them but me. But there you go—I let it go this time; I had no time to do it myself."

The Internet and Free Time

The other area the US study addressed related to home computers and the Internet, and their place in time consumption. In 1995, approximately 35 percent of American households had computers, and the influence of this new technology was the subject of the Times-Mirror Study, conducted by telephone interview, on recall of how the previous day's time was spent. Using these results and expanding the pool of interviewees to accommodate more people who were on the Net, authors Robinson and Godbey found that the total estimated time (40 minutes) on home computers did not create a dent in the use of traditional media (TV, radio). They also noted

> Now, quality time with the kids may mean sitting in front of the computer.

that the use of new media technologies such as the computer tends to generate synergy with the more traditional media. In this case there was a greater time allotment to reading print. Media researchers call this phenomenon "the more, the more." Still, they note, the overall increase in television watching is mostly unaffected by the presence of the home computer.

Not so in Canada, where Statistics Canada, in its year 2000 *General Social Survey*, found that one-quarter of Internet users reported a reduction in their television watching and 15 percent spent less time reading books, magazines, and newspapers. About 10 percent reported that they devoted less time to sleeping, leisure activities, and household chores. (As more men than women use the Internet, this must mean many languishing do-it-your-self projects!)

Computers, with or without an Internet connection, have had a pro-found influence on middle-aged women both in the workplace and at home. Some would argue that this technology has caused more stress, whereas oth-ers would say it has freed up more time (just like those other labor-saving devices!). I suspect the truth is a little more complex than either of these assertions. Certainly, computers and continually changing software applica-tions are a constant source of stress. We all know that there is often not enough on-the-job training, leaving many women trying to teach themselves, often at home and late at night. Now, quality time with the kids may mean sitting in front of the computer.

On the other hand, the Internet has allowed many women to become connected in a manner they could not have foreseen in the 1960s. The use of video and digital technology allows women in remote communities to talk to one another and to resurrect the tradition of oral communication that time and distance have endangered.

Statistics Canada reports that men are more likely to use the Internet than women in every age group. However, women have closed the gap sub-stantially since 1994, when 22 percent of men compared with 14 percent of women were "hooked up." By 2000, the percentage of men on the Net had more than doubled, to 56 percent, while the percentage of women had more than tripled, to 50 percent. Some statistics suggest that women use the Internet mainly for information; for example, 46 percent of Canadian women using the Net do so in order to research medical information.

Will this technology give women greater scope to express themselves to one another, to share information and experiences, or will it be yet another time-cruncher? The jury is still out on the answer for our generation to this question, but I suspect that for our children and grandchildren, being with-out the Internet will be the equivalent of being without a typewriter, a tele-phone, and a television—all rolled into one.

In the end, Einstein probably had it right. You have to accept the idea that subjective time, with its emphasis on the now, has no objective meaning. The distinction between past, present, and future is only an illusion, however persistent.

2

THE CONSEQUENCES
OF TURNING RED

*A sphere is not made up of one, but of an infinite number of
circles; women have diverse gifts and to say that women's
sphere is the family circle is a mathematical absurdity.*

MARIA MITCHELL, 19TH-CENTURY AMERICAN ASTRONOMER

In Chapter 1, the defining issues of middle age were described within the context of two factors: first, the length of time one can actually be said to be in menopause—that process doctors love to refer to as perimenopause (which for the purposes of research applications can start at age 35); and second, the time crunch—that sense of too much to do and little or no time in which to do it, or what I refer to as the middle-aged women's time lament.

> One's prime is exclusive. You little girls, when you grow up, must be on the alert to recognise your prime at whatever time of your life it may occur.
>
> —*Muriel Spark,* The Prime of Miss Jean Brodie

To set the scene for what follows, not only in this chapter but throughout the book, I have here examined both these factors, the issues that make up so much of this personal upheaval, and the physical challenges that we have come to name the menopause.

In the 19th century, the word "menopause" described a process that doctors considered to be a derangement, albeit temporary, or a nervous disorder. Even then, it was acknowledged by physician CF Menville that, "Once they were through it, afflicted women would then enjoy not only a longer life than men but also a mental capacity that had greater precision, more scope, and more vitality than before."

I will illustrate the dance that is the interface between the office practice and the strategies that are suggested by the marketplace where, in their quest for relief, women go to find remedies, often devoting not only numerous hours to information-gathering but also substantial financial outlays. The fact that such an enormous resource of information and alleged solutions exist has always, to my mind, confirmed the notion that there is no quick fix, no immediate remedy, and no universal antidote to the issues inherent in being menopausal. Natural remedies have a long history that remained in the hands of traditional healers and which were passed along in an oral apprenticeship until recently—recently, that is, in the history of Western allopathic (conventional) medicine.

As an MD, it is my job to assess the disturbance that my women patients present, and to sort out what I believe to be, based on my training and experience, a narrowly defined medical pathology and what can be done to remedy the situation. However, as a woman, I have had the opportunity to listen to other women's stories about the wealth of alternative remedies that have been offered and tried; to marvel at the history of medicines, medicants and their usage; and to bridge, as best I can, Western medicine with traditional (now called complementary and alternative) remedies, which my patients actively seek.

In conventional medicine, estrogen is commonly prescribed for relief of menopausal symptoms. So let's examine both the estrogen question—within the larger context of hormone replacement therapy (HRT) and its role during the next few years—and what I consider to be the "big three": moisture (also known as sweats), memory, and mood—the three most common reasons propelling women to the first (but not the last) visit to my office.

ESTROGEN: TO HELL AND BACK AND THEN SOME

They all ask the same questions: "How long will I be on estrogen?" "When are you taking me off estrogen?" and, "Have you read the papers?" "They" are virtually all my menopausal patients who are taking estrogen. They are worried, and they have a right to be. Estrogen is the hormone replacement drug used by millions of women to blunt the most annoying symptoms of menopause. These range from hot flushes (also referred to as flashes), vaginal atrophy, and sleep disturbance to thinning bones, memory loss, heart disease, and maybe even Alzheimer's disease.

By the early 1970s, nearly every woman reaching menopause was being prescribed estrogen, accompanied by the fervent evocation that it would keep them looking young, beautiful, and sexy.

A little bit of history is necessary here to understand this troubled relationship women have with the hormone that makes women, women. Estrogen was once all but abandoned by conventional medicine and, if the volume of negative evidence in the latest studies continues to increase, its commercial popularity may retrace its trajectory of 25 years ago into the cellar.

Premarin, the first and most widely used estrogen preparation, has been around since the early 1940s, when the first studies on animals were conducted by Fuller Albright. Throughout the 1950s and into the '60s a formulation of estrogen and progesterone was created that gave women effective control of their fertility, in the form of the birth control pill. This event coincided with another seminal movement: feminism. Women were now seen to have control of their destiny even though there were enormous pitfalls along the way, one of the biggest being visualizing what that destiny was supposed to look like.

> *Sex appeal is fifty percent what you've got and fifty percent what people think you've got.*
>
> —*Sophia Loren*

In the 1960s, Dr. W. Wilson provided an enormous boost to the prescribing popularity of estrogen "from puberty to the grave" with the publication of his book *Feminine Forever*. According to Wilson, estrogen was the means to erase menopause, by then touted as a deficient state induced by the "flagging" ovaries' declining production of this sex steroid. In other words, it was a state that could be offset with a daily dose of a little red pill. With this simple act, "age-defying youthfulness" characterized by "a straight-backed posture, supple breasts, taut smooth skin on face and neck, firm muscle tone and that particular vigor and grace typical of a healthy woman" was assured to all women who would otherwise sink into "a serious, painful and often crippling disease."

Consequently, by the early 1970s, nearly every woman reaching menopause would be prescribed estrogen by her physician or gynecologist—most of whom were men. Premarin was to menopause what aspirin was to headaches. And it was accompanied by the fervent evocation that it would keep women looking young, beautiful, and sexy. According to the male physicians, Premarin would keep us feminine forever.

Then, in 1975, the *New England Journal of Medicine* was preparing to publish an original research document that suggested women taking

Premarin faced an increased risk of getting cancer of the endometrium (the lining of the uterus) and gall bladder disease. This was the first official hint for the medical community that Premarin might not be the miracle drug its makers and prescribing advocates claimed it was. If the journal's article had appeared simply on its own, it might have languished in the drone of medical debate about how good the study was, or the study's methodology, or its scope. However, in its quest for relevance and modernity, this prestigious medical journal had partnered with *Vogue* magazine, which was to publish articles on any new developments in women's health. The *New England Journal of Medicine* pulled a media coup by advancing a copy of the Premarin article to the women's magazine. When the bad news hit *Vogue* readers, Premarin sales immediately plummeted. The risk of gall bladder disease went unnoticed, but that of endometrial cancer hit a nerve that was both galvanizing and infuriating to the newly sensitized feminist guerillas in America. Within a year, sales of Premarin were down by 75 percent. By 1980, any doctor prescribing estrogen would be met with raised eyebrows.

However, slowly but surely, the sales of Premarin began to rise, until they now dwarf even the prescription rates of the mid-1970s. How did this once discredited drug rehabilitate itself? In the early 1990s, it was confirmed that if Premarin was combined with another hormone replacement drug called progesterone, the risk of endometrial cancer was dramatically reduced. The marketing departments of the pharmaceutical companies outdid their laboratories in repackaging Premarin and all its generic varieties to suit a more skeptical generation of women, women who were much more concerned about their health than their looks. After all, at 60, would you rather be beautiful or not have heart disease? However, because that combination still carried some risk of cancer, doctors were careful to say, "If you have low risk of cancer and want to protect yourself against heart disease or osteoporosis, then by all means take HRT. Even if you have a high risk of cancer, the chances of increasing that risk is not that great, so take it, but use caution."

Consequently, during the 1990s, most doctors in North America were, yet again, prescribing estrogen—now in combination with progesterone—to their menopausal patients. The basis of such a positive view of estrogen was cemented when, in 1992, the Nurses' Study, a landmark study of almost 120,000 American nurses, was reported in the *New England Journal* as showing a 50 percent difference in the incidence of heart disease among women taking the drug compared with those who were not. Considering that one in 10 Canadian women suffers from osteoporosis and that, in Canada, more women than men die of heart attacks, these are not trivial benefits.

However, in 2001, two things happened that began, once again, to shed doubt on estrogen's role as a miracle drug. First, the HERS (Heart and Estrogen/progestin Replacement Study) Trial looked at estrogen and progesterone to deter-mine the protective benefit of hormones in preventing heart disease. The trial met all the criteria that physicians crave: it was (1) ran-domized, meaning that who got which drug, if any, was determined by chance; (2) con-trolled, meaning that participants were sorted by similarities; (3) blinded, in that participants didn't know which drug they were on, if any; and (4), it had power: enough women were involved in the testing to ensure validity. After 4 years of observing more than 4,000 women with heart disease take hormones or placebo, the findings were that taking the drug resulted in no benefits. In fact, it was discovered—almost incidentally—that women on the drug faced a higher, not lower, risk of developing blood clots in the first year of taking hormones. To further confuse matters, the ongoing Nurses' Study, now reporting results after 16 years, pointed to the fact that women taking HRT for 10 years or more faced an increased risk of breast cancer.

> *Back in the 1970s, women took Premarin on their doctor's say-so—no questions asked. Today, they ask questions.*

The results of these two studies, although loudly refuted, have already caused the *Journal of Clinical Practice*, a mainstay publication for Canadian physicians, to shift its practice recommendations. While previously doctors were encouraged to discuss risk-benefits of HRT with patients who had risk for breast cancer, now the advice has firmly swung away from such guidance and does not support the use of hormone replacement where there is risk of breast cancer.

Today, the Nurses' Study is supported by two more recent publications, the first from the US National Cancer Institute, reporting on 46,000 post-menopausal women, and the second, from the National Cancer Institute, on the failure of combination estrogen/progesterone to protect women from the expected breast cancer risk. Nor was it a surprise to the 38,000 cardiologists assembled in New Orleans in the winter of 2001 that the head of the American Cardiology Association stepped away from recommending estrogen as a first-line treatment for women in the war on heart disease.

If this were the 1960s, feminists would by now be beating down the doors of the medical establishment in outrage at the potential harm to the well-being of women. It is perhaps a credit to women today that they are deemed more informed about the limitations of clinical trials to help guide their own decisions and needs. But it leaves them exactly where they were in the 1970s: on their own. The difference is that back then, women took Premarin on their doctor's say-so, no questions asked. Today, they ask questions. Unfortunately, their doctors do not have all the answers.

So, for those women with a family history of breast cancer, or for those who feel uncomfortable adding any new risk for breast cancer, I will turn, in my practice, to many of the alternative strategies and herbal medications that women have used over the years. For menopausal women who want to reduce their risk of heart disease, there are plenty of other drugs available to directly attack their problem, assuming it is an identifiable problem. Lipid-lowering drugs are a big part of that arsenal, as are antihypertensives and smoking-cessation drugs.

It is true that in prescribing such drugs, the physician may be increasing the likelihood of potentially serious side effects. However, it is the job of the prescribing physician to know the selection of pharmaceuticals at his or her disposal, to prescribe yet at the same time enlist the patient in assessing both the good and the bad, the benefit and the risk of these powerful molecules in the medical pharmacopoeia. And when all the talk about drugs is finished, I will always bring my patient back to the work of midlife: walking, weight control, and exercise.

Moisture: The Terminal Flush

The most common condition that drives women to my office seeking relief is the hot flush, or what I call the terminal flush—the living end. We have many euphemisms for this occurrence of disordered physiology: power surges, excess yang, fire from below. Between 85 and 90 percent of women will experience hot flushes as they "go through." Flushes are more or less a nuisance, and they are more or less disruptive to a woman's routine. There are also more or less extenuating circumstances that influence how adaptive women can be in dealing with this disruption.

> *Flushes are more than just a pain when they ride the whirlwind of night arousals: disrupting sleep and causing the broken, nonrestful sleep associated with drenching night sweats.*

Sudden dripping is a problem for a woman if she works where she believes there to be inherent sexism or ageism on the job. Often these women are in highly competitive, stressful jobs, vying with male counterparts for contracts and clients. Sudden redness and dripping sweats, which can overtake in seconds, are embarrassing. For many of these women, their identity is linked to changelessness and the energy of youth, and the veneer of imperturbability is hard to maintain beneath a sheen of sweat or the signaling of their sudden plight as they reach for something with which to furiously fan themselves. "I cannot stand it anymore. You have to do something. I'm soaking through my blouses so badly that I can't take off my jacket in meetings. I'd have to squeeze the water out. And it's happening thousands of times during the day. It's driving me to drink." And, as many of us know, alcohol and caffeine are major triggers for flushing.

The other time flushes are more than just a pain is when they link up with and ride the whirlwind of night arousals: when they disrupt sleep, causing the broken, nonrestful, nonrestorative sleep associated with drenching night sweats. As one of my patients complained, "I'm in bed by 10 o'clock because I'm so tired. Sex is a faint memory of a long ago age. I just want to, need to, get some sleep. But by two in the morning I'm up, I'm down, the covers are off, the covers are on, I'm either freezing or boiling and it happens so fast that I'm not sure if it wakes me up or is causing me to wake up. My husband just gets up and goes to sleep in the next room because I tell him there is no point in changing the linen on two beds. But I'm not a nice person when I'm saying it. Even to myself, I'm a whiny, bitchy, short-tempered shrew. So I'm really grouchy in the mornings and, try as I may, I don't look forward to a classroom of teens that have hormones that are even rockier than mine."

The condition is easy for Western-trained doctors to fix. But by now, we have come to see that that quick fix with estrogen may neither be the best nor the right fix. However, it works, and it works well. So well, in fact, that in drug trials with estrogen, each woman knows if she has been switched off the hormone. Why? Because she starts having hot flushes within three days of when she stops taking the hormone.

The efficacy of estrogen in relieving hot flushes probably depends on where you are in the journey to menopause. Most of my patients who describe these scenarios are still menstruating, many of them quite regularly. What they are experiencing is the fluctuations of hormone levels that can occur as an indicator to the next phase of their lives. Therefore, it might be more helpful to view these incidents as a parallel process similar to that which our teenagers experience—certainly in terms of the emotional roller coaster that besets them and for which we make enormous allowances. We acknowledge that our kids are reacting to the rushes of their hormone surges; we as family members duck and run for cover while we wait for the rush to pass and the daughter or son we know so well to resurface.

Simply understanding that fluctuations of hormone levels are a temporary state rather than a permanent condition may prevent the knee-jerk response that often occurs after starting any hormone regime too soon or before allowing nature enough time to reassert control and bring cycles and moods back in line for another run. Too early a leap to assert control by taking hormones in postmenopausal doses often leads to break-through bleeding—that most often cited reason for discontinuing the hormones. But the alternative, which is to assume control of the entire menstrual cycle with a dose of hormones suited to suspend ovulation (four times the strength used in HRT), does two things that may dissuade women from taking this step. First, it commits physician and patient to medicating the whole of the menopausal transition. Since we do not really know when a woman will in fact become menopausal and cease producing estrogen or progesterone in measurable quantities, we arbitrarily say that at age 52 she may be assumed to be menopausal and at that time her hormone dosage may be reduced to the lower level. I know many a patient, myself included, who continues to have regular periods through to age 55. And then, as my patients say, the periods must surely stop.

Second, and as a result of the educational programs of the early 1990s, women are reluctant to be put on birth control after age 40 even if they are not smokers (smokers older than 35 are no longer prescribed birth control pills because of the increased vascular hazards related to nicotine and hormones). "I haven't taken birth control pills in 15 years," they tell me. "Not since my husband got fixed after our surprise third child. Frankly, I felt much better off them, once I stopped. Do you really thing it's right for me to start again?"

The answer to this question involves a delicate transaction in my office, and the success of the prescription has as much to do with my relationship with my patient as her assessment of her need. What we discuss in the office has to do with choices that women are being asked to make. The decision is theirs, but the information I provide is based not only on what is known scientifically and subject to change but what I know about them and their particular needs. Are there other practitioners out there who can offer equally effective strategies or pathways through this dilemma? Most resoundingly, yes. They abound within the complementary networks in which women look for alternative methods, often in combination with what transpires in my office. D.M. Eisenberg and colleagues reported in the *Journal of the American Medical Association* that between 1990 and 1997 the expenditures for alternative medicine in the United States had increased by an estimated 45 percent and by conservative estimates was placed at US$27 billion in out-of-pocket expenses.[1] Although such a survey has not been done in Canada, the results of such a one would likely parallel the trends that are so evident in our neighbor to the south.

My patients seek naturopaths, homeopaths, and even the wealth of traditional healers. They descend on libraries, search the Internet, share formulas and suggestions. They devour health-related magazines and are enormously open to the escalating market of natural remedies. Yet, even as more and more natural products become standardized in terms of content and purity, there is still a dearth of good clinical trials that demonstrate effectiveness. Some, such as a study of the role of isoflavones found in soy and the relationship to lipids and heart disease, are now being reported. Others have examined the role of St. John's wort and mood disturbance, but these have been mostly small trials, limited in time and duration of study. However, I have little doubt that if St. John's wort is effective in elevating my patient's mood and she feels more comfortable taking this remedy than filling a prescription from me for an SSRI (selective serotonin reuptake inhibitor) then, that's well and good.

> *Even as more and more natural products become standardized in terms of content and purity, there is still a dearth of good clinical trials that demonstrate effectiveness.*

The Arsenal Against the Flush: Herbal Remedies

Many of my patients have reported varying degrees of relief from certain menopausal symptoms by using the herbs I refer to in this chapter. These herbs come in various forms: capsules containing powder, capsules containing a gel extract, capsules containing liquid, and tinctures. Before or while taking any of these preparations, remember to discuss with your doctor and any other practitioners you may be consulting.

The issues arising around flushing and night sweats are not relegated to the back pew by something as easy as consuming quantities of soy. For one thing, the amount of soy recommended in the diet to lessen the frequency and effects of hot flushes is far more than most North American women can imagine consuming. A cake of soy the size of a pound of butter was one of the directives suggested by a master of chi gong. Recently, there has been a move to manufacture a highly concentrated form of soy in capsules, which would provide the same or even greater level of isoflavones, the sought-after element in soy, in an easily ingested way. But this raises questions: Is this natural? Do we need to be concerned about how the body processes this in addition to all the other dietary inclusions?

Dong quai *(Angelica sinensis)* is the other Chinese herb with which most of my patients have some acquaintance. Interestingly, a Chinese patient exclaimed when I suggested she might try dong quai that her mother's generation would brew chicken in a special dong quai cooking pot and drink the broth in order to cleanse the body after monthly menses; its function was to restore the yin.

Other commonly used natural remedies that purportedly offset flushes include black cohosh, red clover, vitamin E, oil of evening primrose (efamol), and gingko biloba (maidenhair tree). Of all these remedies, the most popular seems to be Remifemin, a German-manufactured product containing black cohosh, which is taken in capsular form three to four times daily. At that dosing there may be some tendency to bowel disturbance—a matter for discussion between practitioner and client. Often a combination of products will be advised for relief of the terminal flush.

Further debate arises when the whole arsenal of Chinese medicine is considered alongside the remedies of homeopathy. Popular in Europe for more than 100 years and gaining acceptance in North America, homeopathy treats symptoms with dilutions of substances that in themselves cause symptoms similar to those you are attempting to relieve, based on the hypothesis that like cures like. The remedies that are put together for a suffering menopausal woman are in effect a compilation of her symptoms. So whether it is heat erupting from the middle of her chest and rising like a fireball into her face and neck, leaving a burning sensation and prickliness, or night arousals, leaving her tense and full of restless apprehension, each symptom is addressed with an extremely diluted like-producing toxin. It is the patient listener who can construct the appropriate formulations.

MEMORY LOSS: AN ALARMING PART OF MENOPAUSE

The other day I went to my bank machine to deposit a check. I punched in my personal identification number, signed the check, grabbed an envelope, and looked at the screen. "PIN incorrect. Please try again." At that precise moment, my PIN—the one I've used for 20 years—went missing from my brain. I stared at the screen. It was blank. So was I. I waited. Would the number come back to me? When? Should I walk away? Hit my head? Come back later? I have been in menopause long enough not to panic with this kind of memory lapse, and I share many stories with patients about this very thing.

> *What truly helps is a good sense of humor coupled with the ability to own the lapse and turn it over to the realm of the ridiculous.*

For women who are in early menopause, not only is forgetting things alarming, but remembering things starts to become a real burden. This realization that memory begins to falter in midlife can be especially distressing for the woman who is an investment banker or lawyer or, for that matter, doctor. These occupations put huge demands on memory—the labyrinth of rigid deadlines, cascading commitments, and minute detail—and there can be serious consequences when memory begins to fail. So these professionals, along with other menopausal women, adopt "elaborate" coping strategies to mask their loss of memory, then panic all the more when they cannot remember what that elastic band is doing around their wrist. By the time I see them in my office, they are fearful that others in their organizations will discover their inadequacies and find a way to dismiss them or maneuver them out of highly responsible positions. Some are convinced they have Alzheimer's or, at the very least, that they are in the early days of mental decline.

Reassuring women who believe they are suffering from memory loss is not easy. I have patients so frightened by the thought of being demented like their mothers or grandmothers that they request immediate referral to a psychologist for testing. As it turns out, this strategy offers little reassurance. Most psychologists are unhappy about testing midlife women for this particular problem. They will do it, at no small expense, but most of them will declare that their findings cannot be guaranteed. Since I'm usually looking for a way to reassure my patients that all is well, I'm at a loss to know whether that caveat means, "If the tests say you're okay, you may not be" or "If you're not okay, don't worry, it doesn't mean anything anyway." So I usually discourage women from going this route.

The other quick-fix strategy that most women inquire about is, of course, estrogen replacement, since certain clinical studies show a link between estrogen and the brain receptors that enhance memory. Dr. Barbara Sherwin did most of the early work in this field from Montreal.[2] In those trials that are most-quoted (and certainly in those that are most-marketed), women taking estrogen performed much better on tests of their verbal memory than did those women who were not taking estrogen.

The other seductive image is one we have from animal studies, that of brain neurons (nerve cells) actually growing new dendrites (the parts of a nerve cell that convey impulses to the nerve cell body) when they are bathed in estrogen. The scene looks very busy and very productive, and most of us would like our own brains to be doing that same busy, productive thing. But no one knows for sure yet whether missing estrogen means missing dendrites means missing memory. Further, memory has many more components than rote learning and verbal recall, as all researchers have acknowledged.

Is the memory loss that so often accompanies menopause the same memory loss that afflicts victims of Alzheimer's? No; it is not even close. The nature of what I call "menopause memory loss" is almost always just a lapse, and the only time it becomes more than a brief episode is in the face of anxiety or panic. I can guarantee that if one of my patients misplaces her car keys as she is getting ready to go out the door, she will have an extraordinarily difficult time remembering where she put them. But like as not she will do that woman thing and begin to berate herself about all the other failings of her character, concluding that she is an irresponsible, ineffective, and dithering, failing woman, masquerading as a competent human being.

So here is what truly helps: a good sense of humor coupled with the ability to own the lapse and turn it over to the realm of the ridiculous. The moment slides by, and whatever has been forgotten invariably slides back into place, though often a day or so later and unbidden—a surfacing dolphin of memory if not Moby Dick himself. The other comfort is that which women provide each other by simply sharing their common plight. Through the simple act of saying, "I forgot my boss's name yesterday," they can relieve an enormous amount of anxiety.

As for the effects of waning estrogen levels and memory loss in menopausal women, doctors and researchers need to assess not only verbal and visual memory but also the ways we process and manipulate memory for recall. Add to that the numerous tests that assess attention, information processing, efficiency, and reaction time, and the way to measure or document wisdom and ... well, you get the picture. Defining memory is a complex process. In addition, many clinical trials are now expanding the range of how functioning in the aging process is assessed, and the reporting of the Nun's study provides some heartening insights, as we shall see in Chapter 6.

Ginkgo and Memory

Regardless of the complexities that arise from trying to define what constitutes memory, a waning or absent memory, along with the fear of this, is a perplexing and vexing issue for my patients. They seek help for this with almost the same regularity as for terminal flushes. Ginkgo *(Ginkgo biloba)* is one of those herbs that has its roots in the Far East and has made its way into the natural-remedy pharmacopoeia. Historically, it has been used to improve circulation and is often recommended after strokes to improve circulation to small vessels in the brain as well as vessels in the extremities, and to normalize blood pressure. It is also recommended after concussion.

Certainly, some of my patients have reported that after taking this herb their thinking is sharper and their retention of detail much better. For that reason alone I wouldn't wish to subject them to critical memory testing. Once I have seen a patient take an initiative and note improvement, why would I set out to discredit success? That is the dance of the practitioner, and it is not so much a nod to placebo effect but rather recognition that, as practitioners, we do not know what is truly happening and so we too often discount it as a placebo effect.

Moody Blues

"Don't you discount my anger about this because I'm going to have my period," shouted one of my patients to her long-suffering mate. Three days later, her period came and at its onset her anger totally dissipated. She was not sorry for the heat of her emotions. If anything she was perplexed that she could be so torn up about an issue and then let it go within such a short time. None of my patients like to think she can so easily swing in her emotions about day-to-day household issues. For one thing, it may prove the household's appraisal—that her behavior is being driven by hormones—which in turn leads to the household response—to discount the behavior—which results in discounting the person exhibiting the behavior.

Women, who have struggled and performed with excellence to get to the top of their fields, now find they are peculiarly at risk if there are any unexpected outbursts of emotion. One of my patients was left feeling paranoid about a new job-review process that found her productivity suddenly called into question, even though she had had years of superb reviews. As much as she struggled at work to stay in control, she was more often than not reduced to tears as the process ground her down, and feeling more and more out of control. Her explosion came when she told her supervisor that if there were one more management review of her work, she would be out on stress leave. It was not a threat.

It is true that for some of these women, many years of being long-suffering and patient have earned them a certain right to stand up and shout the now famous *Network* script line, "I'm mad as hell, and I don't have to take it anymore." Indeed, that utterance by Peter Finch is the most frequently quoted line in my office when we are discussing how women may suddenly, out of nowhere, pop off at their loved ones and colleagues. No one is more surprised than these women, who for years have been mastering the art of keeping their anger contained and its expression only warily expressed. They are not thinking differently than they ever have; it's just that they are now more open about their views, less kind, less nice, and less desirous of providing a feel-good cushion.

These are the frequent, explosive, and unwelcome moments many women patients experience on a predictably regular schedule as they make their way through the monthly blues in their 40s. The difference from what they knew in their teens and 20s? Now, the drama is predictable.

Evening Primrose Oil and Serenity

There is probably no greater time-gobbler than the task of helping my patients find methods to control the intense mood swings that are an inherent part of the change. Even if we opt for the quick fix and hormones are prescribed, the follow-up consumes both time and energy. Therefore, it is often at this juncture that the real interface of natural and/or prescriptive comes into play, which is why practitioners (both complementary and allopathic) must acquaint themselves with what other remedies their patients may be taking.

Traditionally, evening primrose *(Oenothera biennis)* oil has been used to treat premenstrual syndrome (PMS) rather than menopausal symptoms. However, because of its usefulness in regulating mood swings due to fluctuations in hormone levels during PMS, evening primrose oil is becoming recognized as useful in addressing these same issues that arise during the change. The active ingredient in primrose oil is gamma-linoleic acid, an essential amino acid that is part of the substrate (material acted upon by an enzyme) to produce serotonin, one of the neurohormones found in the brain. Lack of serotonin is linked to depression (Prozac was the first in a new class of antidepressants—the SSRIs that work by helping maintain levels of serotonin in the brain tissue).

Consequently, it makes sense that increasing the levels of substrate may help the body increase its level of serotonin, without resorting to an antidepressant drug. However, a depressed mood is not the only symptom that afflicts my menopausal patients: agitation, anxiety, a sense of doom, apprehension, restlessness, and fatigue all wend their way along the corridors to my offices.

St. John's Wort and Depression

Currently, the most frequently used natural remedy for depression is St. John's wort *(Hypericum perforatum)*, which is often the starting point for those who feel they must attempt to chemically alter themselves if they are to manage. As I noted earlier, this herb is often used in combination with other herbal products, such as ginkgo biloba, black cohosh, or red clover, in a compounded preparation. As doctors, we are comfortable with the knowledge that St. John's wort is an effective treatment in mild to moderate depression. We are also comfortable to wait on the National Institutes of Health-sponsored study that compares the effects of St. John's wort with SSRIs in moderate to severe depression. But most would not be comfortable prescribing a SSRI while our patients continued to take undisclosed amounts of St. John's wort, since both share the same metabolic pathways in the liver and both are known to interact with other drugs.

Often the doctor's task is to find out just how much of a product a patient is consuming. In Eisenberg's study, it was noted that almost 50 percent of the people using herbal remedies did not consult any practitioner before starting and 72 percent did not tell their physicians about these remedies at any time. With the increased use of these formulations comes more reports of drug interactions, such as serotogenic shock after combining SSRIs with St. John's wort. The possibility of such reactions makes it vitally important that physicians and other "healers" are apprised of what is being taken: both the amount and frequency. In turn, physicians and natural practitioners alike must be prepared to access websites or compendia to familiarize themselves with the potential interactions of the drugs or herbals remedies being ingested by unsuspecting patients or clients.

Chasteberry: Calming the Fire from Below

The chasteberry shrub *(Vitex Angus-Castus)*, which has been in medicinal use for centuries, is a member of the verbena family. Because it functions as a testosterone-blocker, it has been used to suppress sexual desire in both men and women. Monks in the Middle Ages used the fruit of the shrub for the same reason—hence, one of its names: monk's pepper. Now, chasteberry is used for its purported calming effects.

OTHER HERBAL REMEDIES

Ginseng and Energy

Korean and Chinese ginseng *(Panax ginseng)* is unusual in the panoply of menopausal remedies as it is considered by practitioners of Chinese medicine to be a yang, or male balancer, in much the way that dong quai restores yin. I am assured by my Chinese patients that there is little place for this root in the treatment of female troubles. Nevertheless, many women take this herb as a means to energize themselves, improve libido, decrease hot flushes, and boost the immune system.

Valerian and Sleep

Sleep disturbances are tackled by my menopausal patients in diverse ways. I've had patients who have taken Gravol, Tylenol, Nite-all, even alcohol, all before they see me about sleeping medication. The problem is often compounded by their prior use of such substances since many of the women have developed tolerances to them. Consequently, prescribed medication, including sleeping pills, is ineffective at its usual starting dose; more is required.

Valerian *(Valeriana officinalis)* is a herbal remedy often used to improve sleep and most of my patients are familiar with it as a tincture or an infusion or in a tea. It is a very safe remedy for mild sleeping disturbances. However, the real problem with sleep disturbance relates to the length of time that women may be disturbed with nocturnal hot flushes, as it is these drenching sweats that often make sleeping impossible.

BODY WORK: A HOLISTIC APPROACH

Treating and alleviating what are often multiple signs of distress for midlife women is best done by looking at the whole picture rather than frame by frame in piecemeal fashion. A holistic approach is easily incorporated into allopathic medicine, despite what some may say, though this approach does often require the most patience in practice and persistence in maintaining the benefits. The patient herself controls this treatment; no amount of haranguing or cajoling on my part, as her doctor, will do any good.

The patient herself controls the holistic treatment; no amount of haranguing or cajoling on my part, as her doctor, will do any good.

Another and important aspect of complementary medicine relates to such physically based disciplines as reiki and yoga (body work), which impact on both body and mind. The practitioners of yoga, reiki, meditation, chi gong, and tai chi, as well as personal trainers, are all engaged in the art of fashioning body states that are in harmony with, and a source of power and strength for, the acolyte. Each of these arts instills and exemplifies an underlying belief that the harmony and fluidity created with and by the body will mirror that of the mind; that there is no separation between the two. All such disciplines require a significant investment of time and dedication to realize the benefits, though initial improvements, often in breathing and suppleness, can occur quite early in the journey. These results alone will encourage many of my patients to shake loose their dependency on drugs for calming down; they feel empowered by managing the means to a restful sleep.

If there is one great stumbling block women have to trying this approach, it is time. Too little time for themselves, too much pressure to get other tasks done. My patients assure me that if there were even an hour in the day for themselves, they would prefer to sleep. Convincing them that there is an energy gain to be had by putting themselves in the hands of a yoga teacher, or doing an exercise or dance class when they are feeling bagged and still have to get the kids to hockey, is a tough sell. Do I do it? Do I believe it? Absolutely.

Asserting an iota of control over volatile inner forces is the first step along the path and is often the means by which women begin to master the "time-lord."

3

A Good Heart Will See You Through

Above all, do not lose your desire to walk. Every day I walk myself into a state of well-being and walk away from every illness. I have walked myself into my best thoughts and I know of no thought so burdensome that one cannot walk away from it. But by sitting still, and the more one sits still, the closer one comes to feeling ill ... If one just keeps on walking everything will be all right.

Søren Kierkegaard

The landmark study of the health of a population was and still is the Framingham Heart Study (see p. 55), which started in 1948 in the town of Framingham, Massachusetts, and in which more than 5,200 of its inhabitants were enrolled. A second generation was added in 1971 (the Framingham Offspring Study), and non-whites were included in 1995. The study, which continues to report its findings, even after 50 years, has formed the foundation of all we know about heart disease in men and women. Concepts such as risk factors and the contributory effects of smoking and hypertension entered our consciousness because of Framingham. The data collected have enhanced our views about dementia, osteoporosis, stroke, cancer, and the genetic patterns of many common diseases. But most of all, it is in relation to heart disease that people acknowledge the enormous influence of Framingham.

Framingham documented the onset of heart disease as being 10 years later in women than in men, and this led to the mistaken premise that women, unlike men, do not suffer from heart disease. As a result of this incorrect or at the very most, partially correct, assumption, there have been astonishing differences in heart disease treatment for men and women. The failure to recognize that there are differences between how the two sexes experience their heart disease events plagues us even today, though it is easy to appreciate that women do indeed exhibit unusual or atypical symptoms, which can make diagnosis problematic for the clinician. Because of this, women still have nowhere near the volume or variety of diagnostic procedures that are offered to men.

Some of these more gender-specific patterns are now commonly recognized. For example, a woman's first event is more likely to be angina—chest pain that comes from decreased blood flow to the vessels of the heart. A man's first encounter, on the other hand, is more likely to be a heart attack. Many women experience what doctors refer to as atypical chest pain. It can be in the shoulder or the arm, rather than in the chest; or it can feel like heartburn; or it can occur at times not commonly associated with heart attacks and not necessarily during manual work or physical exertion. When women seek treatment, they are also more likely to be sicker than men and have more co-morbid illnesses (add-on health problems), such as diabetes. Women also are more likely to die from their first heart attack, a consequence not only of being both older and sicker but also of waiting too long before seeking help. ("I waited until my husband came home to take me to the hospital," said one of my patients.) Women are more likely than men to suffer another heart attack within the first year and are less likely to avail themselves of a cardiac rehabilitation program. Also, women who weight cycle, that is, have repeated episodes of weight loss and gain, are at increased risk for coronary disease and mortality.

A number of questions are repeatedly asked in my office, and in answering them, recurrent themes are revealed. Before addressing those questions, however, there are some things you need to know.

Cholesterol, a fatty substance mainly made in the body by the liver, plays a vital role in the functioning of every cell wall throughout the body and is the material by which the body makes other vital chemicals and hormones. However, too much cholesterol in the blood—elevated cholesterol—can increase the risk of coronary heart disease as a result of fatty plaques blocking the blood vessels. A portion of the cholesterol is HDL cholesterol. It is associated with a high-density lipoprotein core and is termed the "good" or "protective" cholesterol. HDLs return excess cholesterol to the liver. Treatments aim at increasing the HDL cholesterol and decreasing the LDL (low-density lipoprotein, which carries cholesterol from the liver to the cells of the body). Often an increase in physical activity is sufficient to raise the HDL cholesterol.

Elevated cholesterol along with electrocardiogram (ECG) abnormalities (an ECG is a test done to record the rhythm and activity of the heart) became acknowledged risk factors for heart disease. In 1974, the association of diabetes, a disease caused by a lack of insulin or an increased resistance of body cells to insulin, and its attendant complications, were outlined by the Framingham Study as a risk factor for heart disease. Maturity-onset diabetes is often associated with high cholesterol and high triglycerides (fatty substances found in the blood) as well as high blood sugar.

In 1976, menopause was added to the growing list of risk factors for heart disease.

Should I Worry About This Pain in My Chest?

Because of the new consciousness of heart health for all women, my patients have now begun to appreciate that they may not be immune to heart prob-lems. Trouble is, they often don't know how to read the signs, and sometimes they are put onto a firing line, perhaps needlessly. My 48-old patient told me the following story.

> *No chest pain should be ignored or discounted until all the facts have been gathered for consideration.*

One afternoon, while grocery shopping and rushing to get home to make dinner, she started to experience chest pain. The pain began as a dull aching sensation in her midchest and gradually built in inten-sity until she couldn't think about anything except getting home. Which she did—by driving there. Her husband, upon hearing of her symptoms, put her back in the car and drove her to the hospital. In the emergency room, she was hooked up to monitors, blood was taken, a history was obtained, she was given medication. She remained in the hospital for 48 hours before being sent home, after being told that she had no cardiac problem. What was missing after this $4,800 workup was any explanation of her symptoms, especially as she had exercised flawlessly on the treadmill during the obligatory stress cardiogram before being discharged. For answers and to try to make sense of her symptoms, she had come to get my opinion. She did have an explanation, and it made sense, but only after the overriding anxiety of whether she had a heart problem was put to rest.

This approach—off to the hospital, investigations, confirmation that your heart is in good shape—may not be necessary for everyone, especially if they are reasonably exercised and know they are capable of hard cardiac work without chest pain. But along with exercise must be some understanding of the role played by the stresses of daily life: too much rushing, too quick a meal, or the wrong meal eaten on the run. A history of heartburn, or a fat intolerance, or a touchy digestion must also be taken into account. All of these things applied to my patient. As she herself noted, while she was happy for the reassurance from the hospital, she felt the whole process was excessive given that no problem was found. That sentiment reflected, more than anything, her embarrassment at the bother she felt she had put everyone through. In the end I'm not sure that she would have been so completely reassured without all the investigations, and she gained a big boost to her confidence by being able account for her symptoms.

Today, many more women will be referred for stress cardiograms (walking increasingly faster on a treadmill in order to accelerate heart rate and cardiac workload) in an effort to uncover heart damage or ischemia (inadequate blood supply). Since women may manifest their heart conditions in unusual ways, often mistaking the symptoms for heartburn or anxiety or palpitations, these tests may not be conclusive, which is when healthy suspicion must be given its due. For example, questions about other risk factors, such as smoking or diabetes, should be asked. This is where family doctors have the added advantage of knowing their patients.

The answer to the question of whether to ignore chest pain is that no chest pain should be ignored or discounted until all the facts have been gathered for consideration. This is not a bother; it is good medicine. The most difficult thing sometimes is to help women assess the nature of the pain rather than simply ignore it or be frightened out of their wits by it.

MY FAMILY HAS A TERRIBLE HEART HISTORY; WHAT DO I NEED TO KNOW?

Many of my patients come from families with poor heart histories and are genuinely concerned about what they need to know. Providing some real reassurances can be most helpful.

A 50-something patient explained how her mother had had three heart attacks before she reached 60. My patient was concerned because she didn't want to go on hormone replacement therapy but she was mindful of the press that purported the drug's benefits in counteracting heart disease. Inquiry revealed that her mother had been a lifelong smoker, overweight, and had never exercised. The patient, on the other hand, was perhaps 10 pounds above ideal weight, and a nonsmoker. These two facts alone, with regard to what we know to be modifiable factors, have a much larger impact on the potential risk of heart disease than the apparent familial pattern bequeathed by her mother. Even allowing for the contribution of such familial patterns as hyperlipidemia (an excessive amount of cholesterol in the blood) and diabetes, the life choices people make can override the seemingly inevitable consequences. So assessment is required of the truly modifiable risk factors. These we know are diabetes, hypertension, hyperlipidemia, sedentary life style, being overweight, and smoking.

> *Diabetes is a particularly important risk factor in women; its presence in women is associated with a greater risk of coronary heart disease than is its presence in men.*

For diabetics, excellent control of blood sugar has become the goal for which they and their doctors aim. Better blood sugar control means better cholesterol and triglyceride levels and, therefore, less plaque development in coronary vessels. If such control can be accomplished with diet alone, well and good. However, if medication is required, drugs are available that will ensure excellent control of blood sugar. And within the next decade, new treatments that will stimulate the pancreatic production of insulin will evolve. As well, devices that read and deliver the required doses of insulin on an automatic feedback system are in development, so radical changes are anticipated in the near future.

Hypertension, aptly named "the silent killer," has long been a recognized hazard for heart disease and stroke. There are familial as well as racial patterns to rising blood pressure. The good news is that treatment that is initiated in a timely fashion will prevent not only heart damage but also kidney damage.

ABNORMAL STRESS CARDIOGRAMS

One day, a patient of mine was undergoing a stress test when she was asked to step off the treadmill and go to my office. She walked the three or so blocks from the testing office to my office without any information other than that future testing was necessary. We needed to reassure ourselves that she was not in immediate danger. She was not experiencing any discomfort, shortness of breath, or pain while walking on the treadmill or to my office. But her cardiogram had changed while she was exercising—a common occurrence with women. When this happens to men, it usually means they have underlying coronary disease. The same is not true for women, which makes the diagnosis of heart disease even more problematic.

> *To wear your heart on your sleeve isn't a very good plan; you should wear it inside, where it functions best.*
>
> *—Margaret Thatcher*

Often, we can provide an opinion and advice after repeated testing with more elaborate tests that involve the injection of radioactive isotopes (these isotope markers are not picked up by damaged heart muscle so they help us estimate the nature or extent of damage) while the patient undergoes the same stress tests. So, after my patient underwent such tests, I referred her to a hospital cardiologist. Under the cardiologist's supervision, she would have the option of nuclear scans and, if necessary, an even more invasive test: an angiogram (an X-ray of the blood vessels showing both the location and the extent of possible arterial narrowing) to outline the actual vessels supplying the heart.

In the meantime, what does my patient need to do? Some guidelines on what she should watch for and when to be concerned seemed in order. She is a nonsmoker with normal blood pressure, reasonably fit, and not overweight. All this is in her favor. I prescribed her with some nitroglycerine pills and instructed her on how, why, and when she should take them. I advised her to get to the hospital if she experienced unremitting pain or shortness of breath. Part of our discussion involved asking if she had a support network. With whom would she be sharing this information and concern? My patient is single and lives alone, so it is vital to know who she has as a buddy. In this case, it is her mother, who is fortunately still capable and independent and available as a back-up for her daughter.

Cardiac Surgery

Many of my patients ask me why is there a waiting list for cardiac surgery in Canada. What a hot potato this is! Is the waiting list a result of resources being too strapped? Is it, as many American doctors say to my patients who visit south of the border, a reflection of socialized medicine with its limited options? Or is it a reflection of supply creating demand: The more you have, the more you do, the more you say you have to do? And is it a political land mine? You betcha!

Not so long ago, a patient was traveling to Hilton Head, South Carolina, for a golfing holiday. She felt some chest pain and stopped in at a small Tennessee hospital deep in the Great Smoky Mountains. A quickly arranged angiogram revealed blockage of her coronary arteries, and she underwent angioplasty, in which a balloon catheter was threaded into the blocked artery, then inflated to open a channel through the blockage. The very next day, she was on the road again, giving a whole new meaning to the model of the "new" care, based on the latest knowledge. It was "care on your feet," or, don't lie down—you are not going to be here that long. "Get yourself a cardiologist when you get home," the surgeon said as she left.

In Canada, this process would have taken five or six office visits and a pre-operation, or pre-op, appointment, before admission into the hospital's catheterization laboratory. If the pain is severe, acute, and sudden, that time frame will be reduced, but the process will inevitably require more time than was experienced by my patient. But is that bad medicine? Is there a problem with that three- to nine-month wait; that is, does such a wait pose a danger? A number of years ago, an international study in the treatment of coronary vessel disease compared the use of coronary artery bypass surgery as opposed to the use of drugs alone. It found that Canadians commonly had drug treatment whereas Americans more often underwent surgical procedures, having more resources for this option. Indeed, the percentage of Canadians undergoing drug treatment was approximately equal to that of Americans having surgery. No difference was found in mortality or recurrence between the two groups. The only difference found was that those treated with drugs alone reported more angina.

Americans have stepped up their demand for cardiac surgery, creating the supply line in doing so. However, in Canada, there aren't enough surgeons to meet the demand. If we look at the percentage increase in the number of procedures between America and Canada, it becomes clearer. Between 1981 and 1987, there was a 108 percent increase in the number of CABG (coronary artery bypass graft) procedures performed in the United States, compared to a mere 39 percent increase in Canada.

> *Between 1981 and 1987, there was a 108 percent increase in the number of coronary artery bypass grafts performed in the United States, compared to a mere 39 percent increase in Canada.*

However, according to a recent Canadian study, there may be other factors to consider as the waiting times lengthen. Quality of life, the incidence of stroke while waiting for surgery, and the failure to be able to return to meaningful employment are all issues that have been shown to be affected in a negative way as the wait extends. Being able to return people to the workplace is an enormous consideration if we are to assess the real cost-benefit of coronary surgery and its availability.

EXERCISE AND HEART DISEASE

The Exercise Prescription

A sedentary lifestyle or inactivity has been studied as a risk factor for coronary disease and is, in itself, equivalent to the "big three" risk factors of hypertension, smoking, and hypercholesterolemia.[1] A number of studies have confirmed that even modest increases in activity enhance cardiovascular health. This has led the National Institutes of Health Consensus Conference on Physical Activity and Cardiovascular Health to call for people of all ages to include a minimum of 30 minutes of physical activity of moderate intensity (e.g., brisk walking at a 15- to 20-minute-per-mile pace) on most if not all days of the week.[2] (A 15-minute-per-mile pace is equivalent to 31.5 kilojoule per minute in terms of energy used. Vigorous activities will consume upwards of 8,400 kilojoule per week.[3]) The greatest gains have been documented in those going from unfit to the lowest levels of fitness.[4]

> *You would need to walk for 87 minutes at 3.5 mph (5.5 km/h) to work off the energy provided by an order of medium-sized fries or a single scoop of soft ice cream.*

Cardiac Rehabilitation

After complaining of a chest pain that wakened her at night, a patient underwent a thorough cardiac investigation. She was diagnosed with multiple vessel blockages, or "small vessel disease," a kind of vessel disease that affects women more often than men. It is not possible to dilate her vessels with balloons or bypass blockages with vessels taken from other parts of the body. Rather, her rehabilitation program consists of the use drugs as a foundation and an exercise program to assist her in developing more and new vessels around the blockages, that is, a collateral circulation. Such programs also include dietary advice, emotional support for the patient and family, and teaching the "smarts" of exertion, capacity, and endurance, so that patients can leave the role of patient behind. If the program is done well and is successful, this patient will probably be fitter, stronger, and more physically capable than she was before she began the program. She will have a better diet, likely weigh less, and have more energy; and her family will cease to be afraid for her.

> *A number of studies have confirmed that even modest increases in activity enhance cardiovascular health.*

But, and it is a big but, we know that women who have been diagnosed with heart disease do not utilize rehabilitation programs in the same way or with the same frequency as men. In fact, one study found that only 5 percent of women actually received rehabilitation services.[5] Many explanations have been cited, including the oft-repeated reason that women need to be home to care for their husbands and families. The truth is probably that women just do not do not allow enough time for themselves, even when their health is in jeopardy. However, we do know that, for whatever reason, compared with men, women do not embrace cardiac rehabilitation with the same vigor. Consequently, a concerted effort is now being made to explain the rehabilitation program to women and advocate its benefits, which includes the comfort of having hospital personnel as trainers, so that women will be encouraged to use the program. A typical program involves eight stations through which women course, with a set amount of time on each machine, including a stair, treadmill, rowing, or ellipse machine. Many women describe the program as rigorous, and they love it. They also acknowledge that it is the support and encouragement of the staff that enables them to reach and often exceed the set goals. Such programs have demonstrable benefits in reducing readmission-to-hospital rates, enabling a faster return to work, improving morale, and reducing overall health care costs for procedures such as bypass surgery and angioplasty. For example, the Dean Ornish Lifestyle program, which combines an exercise program with a low-fat vegetarian diet and stress-reduction techniques, has demonstrated the actual reversal of coronary vessel plaque in a small number of patients.

The notion that women would not achieve a training effect comparable to men's was refuted in a Toronto study of more than 500 matched men and women who performed equally well in a 12-month progressive walking program.[6] The Toronto Cardiac Rehabilitation program under Dr. Terry Cavanaugh now boasts an encouraging 25 percent female participation rate in a plan that addresses their special needs. For instance, since women typically have less aerobic power than men when starting the program, their program is less intense and of shorter duration. To avoid injuries, resistance training starts with light weights, between one-half and one kilogram (from two to three pounds), and women are educated about high-energy-consumption household tasks, such as vacuuming.

Diet and Heart Disease

The Role of Red Wine

There is an ongoing debate about the things we eat and drink. Most often patients want reassurance that it's okay to drink alcohol in the amounts that they currently imbibe. To comfort themselves, they quote the typical French diet, with its emphasis on red wine and cheese, and the apparently lower incidence of heart disease in the French compared with North Americans.

In 1997, a study reported in *Clinical Cardiology* looked at a flavonoid called resveritrol in red wines. This chemical, present in larger quantities in red wines than in whites (except champagne), was thought to be the protective agent because it acts as an antioxidant. And anything that is an antioxidant is thought to be useful in reducing the risk of atheromatous (fatty) plaque disruption in blood vessels. This is in addition to the overall positive effect of alcoholic beverages raising HDL lipids and, possibly, reducing the generation of fibrin, a blood product that may cause the production of clots. Obviously, though, too much alcohol consumption will reverse any benefits and lead to a rise in coronary problems, damage to the liver, and an increase in weight, at the very least.

Omega-3 Oils and Heart Health

The other dietary nugget is the role of omega-3 oils (found in coldwater fish but not shellfish) in the diet. These oils belong to the unsaturated fat group that is beneficial in reducing the total load of the unhealthy saturated and oxidized fats, along with free radicals and trans fats. Antioxidant properties of food groups are thought to be helpful in the prevention of a build-up of atheromatous plaque in blood vessels, since it is the oxidation of LDL (bad) cholesterol that produces the atherosclerotic plaque.

The DART (Diet and Reinfarction Trial) supports the recommendation to have two servings of baked, broiled, or poached fish a week as an alternative to meat.[7]

The DART (Diet and Reinfarction Trial) supports the recommendation that to get healthy omega-3 oils into your diet, you should have two servings a week of baked, broiled, or poached fish instead of meat.

Vitamin E and the HOPE Trial

The value of vitamin E, that time-honored dietary supplement for the mature, with its assumed beneficial effect in preventing heart disease, was critically appraised in a 1999 multicentered study called the HOPE (Heart Outcomes Prevention Evaluation) trial. The study looked at 9,297 patients, some on vitamin E and some on placebo. The results of the vitamin E analysis showed no difference in the actual incidence of coronary heart disease between the groups.

Dietary Fat and Cholesterol

What's all this business about fat, and which is the bad fat? It is true the average North American diet is made up of 30 percent fat, and while some of this fat is obvious, like that in a hamburger and butter, some of it isn't so obvious, like that in granola and nuts.

It was the Framingham study that, in 1961, once again first revealed the effect of blood fat (lipidemia) in the form of elevated cholesterol as a coronary risk factor in developing atheromatous plaques in vessels. We

One pound of fat is equal to 3,500 kcal, so reducing 500 kcal per day will enable a maximum four-pound (1.8 kg) weight loss per month.

have spent 40 years clarifying the differences between HDL (good) and LDL (bad) cholesterol. The data we now seek by doing a HDL/cholesterol ratio after a 12-hour fast allow us to rank a patient's risk for heart attacks and angina compared with the population at large. From such data, guidelines have been assembled for the treatment of these blood-fat levels so that there is a reduction in risk of potential coronary events.

Recently, even bigger studies, involving thousands of high-risk individuals, have shown the benefit of lowering these lipid levels, even in those who do not have evidence of heart disease but who do have elevated blood lipids. By lowering the LDL cholesterol level with drugs called statins (the class of drug used to reduce cholesterol levels), there was a documented 30 percent reduction in coronary deaths, heart attacks, and the need for bypass surgery.[8] (I discuss statins in more detail below.)

And, having spent years and billions of dollars in raising our awareness about cholesterol and HDLs and LDLs, along comes the new kid on the block: apolipoprotein-a. Actually, it is not such a new player and is only one of many other lipoproteins that play a part in the genesis of atheromatous plaque. The notion that there may be one thing that we can measure like apolipoprotein-a or homocysteine (a new addition to our vocabulary of proteins or amino acids) that will indicate the degree of our risk for heart disease is enormously appealing. However, like all new theories, it also serves to remind us that there will always be something else to consider and in all likelihood there will always be more than one factor at play.

One major consideration in preventing and treating heart disease is the food we put into our mouths. The foundation of treatment as far as food is concerned rests on dietary changes and adherence to general principles.

Here is the ideal distribution of calories in your diet:

Total fat   < 30% total calories

Saturated fats   < 10% total calories

Carbohydrates   > 55% total calories

Protein   > 15% total calories

Although we all need some fat in our diet to survive, most of us eat too much fat. Fat can clog up the arteries, leading to heart attack or stroke. The average calorie consumption is 1,800 to 2,400 calories, for both women and men. To have less than 30 percent in the form of fat means that the average daily diet should have no more than 60 to 75 grams of fat per day. And a tea-spoon (5 ml) of any kind of fat, be it butter or oil, contains 5 grams. So one-half of your daily intake of fat can be had by having that Quarter Pounder with Cheese combo from Mcdonald's (35 grams of fat). Compare this to the six-inch Subway Club, at 3.9 grams fat. Muffins, those quickie breakfast-on-the-run pop-its weigh in at 20 grams. By cutting back on animal fat, switch-ing to healthier vegetable fat, and eating lots of fiber, you can stop or even reverse fat build-up in your arteries and reduce your total cholesterol.

The Mediterranean diet emphasizes increasing the amount of fresh fruits and vegetables and using monounsaturated fats such as olive oil and fish oils, thereby lowering the amount of trans-fatty acids in the diet. This can be achieved dramatically in the North American diet by simply cutting out three dietary sources:

> *One in three women needs to lower her cholesterol.*

butter and hard margarine, fatty meats, and high-fat dairy products. But then it wouldn't be the North American diet would it?[9]

How much fat in your diet is okay? The Heart and Stroke Foundation recommends that fat should equal no more than 30 percent of your total daily calorie intake. For women 19 to 74 years old, who should be eating 1,800 to 2,000 calories a day, that means 65 grams (13 teaspoons) or less of fat per day. Here are some simple ways to cut unhealthy (saturated) fat from your diet:

Eliminate: Pick a food that's high in fat, like potato chips, and eliminate it from your shopping cart.

Reduce: Use spreads and salad oils moderately; reduce the size of your meal's portion of meat.

Substitute: Try air-popped popcorn (no topping) instead of potato chips; skinless broiled chicken instead of fried.

Make one low-fat change at a time. Once your taste buds have adjusted, make another change.

The Heartsmart™ Fat-Buster Chart

Instead of	Use	Reduce Fat by up to*
Whole milk	2%, 1%, or skim	9 g per 250 ml (1 cup)
Coffee cream	Milk	10 g per 500 to 750 ml (2 to 3 cups)
Ice cream	Low-fat frozen yogurt, sherbet, or fruit ice	6 g per 125 ml (1/2 cup)
Cheddar cheese	Skim-milk or fat-free cheese	6.6 g per 21 g (3/4 oz)
Sour cream	Low-fat yogurt	21 g per 125 ml (1/2 cup)
Croissant	English muffin or bagel	10.5 g
Granola cereal	Bran Flakes and dried apricots	6 g per 30 g (1 oz) cereal and 5 g (1 tsp) dried apricots
Butter on bread	Jam	6 g per 7 ml (11/2 tsp)
Regular salad dressing	Low-calorie salad dressing	12 g per 15 ml (3 tsp)
Regular beef	Lean beef	5 g per 90 g (3 oz)
Tuna packed in oil	Tuna in packed in water	6 g per 125 ml (1/2 cup)
Bologna	Sliced turkey	21 g per 90 g (3 oz)
Chicken with skin	Skinless chicken	5 g per 120 g (4 oz) chicken breast

* 5 grams of fat is equivalent to 1 teaspoon (5 ml) of fat.
Source: The Fat Buster Chart © 2001, The Heart and Stroke Foundation of Canada

How Do Statins Work?

For people with elevated cholesterol (in particular, their LDL component), the benefits of dietary modification by reducing saturated fats (steaks, crispy chicken skin, cream cheese) has been modest. It does not help that the average North American diet consists of between 30 and 35 percent fat and most of that may be hidden in the foods we eat. Enter the statins, a class of drugs that are much easier for patients to take than previous medications and which provide reductions of up to 30 percent in measured total and LDL (bad) cholesterol levels. A landmark Scandinavian study, the 4-S study, clearly demonstrated the benefits of reducing relative risk of death from heart attacks (it was 42 percent lower in the treated group) when the LDL (bad) cholesterol levels were lowered in people with high LDL and established heart disease.[10]

Researchers have asked, "How many do you need to treat to prevent one event?" It is called the NNN, the number needed to treat, and is a measure of how effective treatments are in preventing diseases. So for the statins, the magic number is 13. That is to say, you have to treat 13 people with elevated LDL cholesterol for five years to prevent a second coronary event even in one of them.[11] It is no wonder that we continue to look for simpler measures like diet control and exercise to help offset medical treatments.

More importantly, since we know that the average cholesterol level in heart attack survivors is only slightly elevated, at 5.4 mmol/L (the ideal is a constantly shifting 5.2 mmol/L), we have to ask if everybody will realize the same benefit by being treated with statins, no matter what their level of LDL cholesterol. Put another way, how cost-effective is the lowering of LDL cholesterol by the use of statins in offsetting future coronary events? And who, in the final analysis, is footing the bill? These questions remain to be answered.

SEEKING HELP FOR YOUR MOTHER

How Do I Get My Mother to Take Her Heart Problems Seriously?

The number of men referred to cardiac rehabilitation programs is five times that of women. The reasons for this are many and varied, from mom being too frail or too sick to her having to look after dad, who is also frail and sick. Or maybe she can't get the connection between being on a treadmill and being able to clean the house without that "dammed heaviness" on her chest. Or she'll ask you what is the bother—she's old already and will just slow down some more. However, women are just as likely to benefit from the program as men, and considering that they are older, frailer, and sicker, it is enormously beneficial to their ongoing well-being. Talk about a new lease!

The mother of one of my patients was finally persuaded to attend the cardiac rehabilitation program for women run by the hospital. She had been a manual laborer all her life and, in addition, there was a language barrier that made it difficult to interpret the data in a way that made sense to her. As well, she was looking after her ailing husband. But her anginal pain wouldn't let up and even she acknowledged that she couldn't keep up with her usual workload. She, who had worked hard all her life, needed to be persuaded that a program of physical work was in fact going to be of some use. But once persuaded, she undertook to train in her own most remarkable way. After her medication was adjusted and she was enrolled in the program, she found her way back to an even higher level of endurance and did so without pain. She was impressed!

> *While the number of men referred to cardiac rehabilitation programs is five times that of women, women are just as likely to benefit from such programs.*

How Do I Get My Mother's Doctor to Take Her Heart Complaints Seriously?

This question really addresses the whole relationship women have with their doctors. Even raising the issue implies that I, as a doctor, am listening to and taking this daughter's question seriously. Most often, my job at this point is to cull the information from the daughter and help frame her concerns and issues. For example, the mother of one of my patients was experiencing clear symptoms of angina, with chest heaviness, constriction, and pain radiating into her jaw with greater and greater frequency. Her mother, though, seemed determined to deny the progression of her symptoms and was reluctant to make an appointment with her doctor. By simply clarifying the escalation of frequency and intensity of her mother's discomfort and what this might mean, the daughter was in a better position to inform and seek guidance from her mother's doctor. The same would be true if the circumstances were concerning her mother's evolving tremor or a failing memory.

Often, I will suggest the two or three issues that need to be addressed so that an accompanying family member has a clear plan of what to focus on going into the doctor's appointment. And yes, daughters, do attend these appointments. Unlike those attended with your teens, where you are invited to wait outside, these appointments work because daughters are invited in. It is often necessary to outline for the doctor what supports exist in the home or need to be put in place to secure the right attention for your mother's problems. A clear message of what is available in the way of family resources is essential for decent planned care.

Much work remains before we have a clearer and perhaps more holistic picture of women's heart health. As women live longer, we need more study of both the physical and socioeconomic effects of such longevity and what role our hearts play. In the meantime, we do have some good basic building blocks of information (stop smoking, eat better—which often means less—and exercise) from which we can form personal heart health strategies.

Framingham Study Milestones

1948

Start of the Framingham Heart Study.

1956

Findings on progression of rheumatic heart disease reported.

1959

Factors that increase the likelihood of heart disease found.

Some heart attacks discovered to be "silent" (causing no pain).

1960

Cigarette smoking found to increase the risk of heart disease.

1961

Cholesterol level, blood pressure, and electrocardiogram abnormalities found to increase the risk of heart disease.

1965

First Framingham Heart Study report on stroke.

1967
Physical activity found to reduce the risk of heart disease and obesity to increase the risk of heart disease.

1970
High blood pressure found to increase the risk of stroke.

1971
Framingham Offspring Study begins.

1974
Overview of diabetes, its complications, and association to development of cardiovascular disease described.

1976
Menopause found to increase the risk of heart disease.

1977
Effects of triglycerides and LDL and HDL cholesterol described.

1978
Psychosocial factors found to affect heart disease.
Atrial fibrillation (a condition in which the heart beats irregularly) found to increase the risk of stroke.

1981
Filter cigarettes found to give no protection against coronary heart disease.
Major report issued on relationship of diet and heart disease.

1983
Reports on mitral valve prolapse (which causes a backward leak of blood between heart chambers).

1986
First report on dementia published.

1987
High blood cholesterol levels found to correlate directly with risk of death in young men.
Fibrinogen (allows blood to clot more easily) found to increase the risk of heart disease.

Estrogen replacement therapy found to reduce risk of hip fractures in post-menopausal women.

1988
High levels of HDL cholesterol found to reduce risk of death.

Association of type "A" behavior with heart disease reported.

Isolated systolic hypertension found to increase risk of heart disease.

Cigarette smoking found to increase risk of stroke.

1990
Homocysteine (an amino acid) found to be possible risk factor for heart disease.

1993
Mild isolated systolic hypertension shown to increase risk of heart disease.

Major report predicts survival after diagnosis of heart failure.

1994
Enlarged left ventricle (one of two lower chambers of the heart) shown to increase the risk of stroke.

Lipoprotein (a) found as possible risk factor for heart disease.

Risk factors for atrial fibrillation described.

Apolipoprotein E found to be possible risk factor for heart disease.

1995
First Framingham report on diastolic heart failure published.

OMNI Study of Minorities starts.

1996
Progression from hypertension to heart failure described.

1997
Cumulative effects of smoking and high cholesterol on the risk for atherosclerosis reported.

Impact of an enlarged left ventricle and risk for heart failure in asymptomatic individuals investigated.

1998
New risk prediction formulas to calculate a patient's risk for developing coronary disease over the next 10 years published.

4

WHAT'S HOLDING YOU UP
CAN LET YOU DOWN

Your bones,
round rulers, round nudgers, round poles,
numb nubkins, the sword of sugar.
I feel the skull, Mr. Skeleton, living its
own life in its own skin.

ANNE SEXTON, "THE FURY OF BEAUTIFUL BONES"

A few years back, I undertook to do research on how women make up their minds about hormone replacement therapy. The research took the form of 10 interviews with groups of 10 or 12 midlife women held during the summer of 1997. One of the fascinating concerns that emerged from those sessions was the women's shared desire to maintain their independence as they aged. What worried them far more than weak hearts, arthritis, or even breast cancer, for that matter, was fracturing their bones and becoming bedridden or dependent.

The projected statistics on Canada's aging population are not reassuring. The incidence and societal costs of hip fractures in the frail elderly is predicted to become an enormous burden in the foreseeable future. Postmenopausal white women account for almost 75 percent of the total number of hip fractures, and allowing for age, they have the highest incidence of *all* fractures. Further, the occurrence of one vertebral fracture predisposes women to a second vertebral fracture within the year—this in spite of calcium and vitamin D supplementation.

While there is enormous benefit in turning the responsibility for the prevention of osteoporotic fractures over to the women who are at risk, the tools to ensure that they can accomplish this are not quite in place. Consequently, the burden of worrying about something 30 years in advance, a scenario that is known to all women, is dropped into the lap of midlife women along with all the other vestments of menopause. The questions and issues discussed in this chapter come not from my 70-year-old patients but from the 50 year olds who are concerned about bone density, dietary calcium, and fracture risk, issues they perceive as potential threats to independence during their old age. Everyone can relay the story of Grandma or Great Aunt Sue, whose seemingly innocuous slip and tumble resulted in a broken hip. Therefore, everyone can relate to the consequences of the 25 percent who die as a result of complications, the 25 percent who are unable to leave hospital, and the 25 percent who cannot continue to maintain their independence.

As a result, the prevention and management of this fearsome condition become important, for both the public health system and the women who likely need most of those thinly stretched resources, those scanty tools of pre-vention—aging women. The time to be concerned is not when you are turn-ing 50 but when you and now your children are young: pediatric neglect, geriatric outcome. Dietitians have found that many young women consume only about one-third of the recommended daily dietary intake of calcium, and the reason for this is that they don't want the extra calories.

When she is 50 years of age, a woman's lifetime risk for an osteoporotic-related fracture is one in two. Genetics plays about a 75 percent role in determining if bones are strong, the other 25 percent rests with bone loss following menopause, aging, and all things that predispose women to falling. The projection for the Canadian health care system is that 40 years from now, we will be dealing with four times the number of fractures that we are currently experiencing. All industrialized nations with an aging population are being propelled to examine this as a public health issue that requires intervention now rather than down the road.

HOW DO I PREVENT OSTEOPOROSIS?

First, a definition: Osteoporosis is the abnormal loss of bony tissue, causing fragile bones that fracture easily, often without an injury being noted; pain, especially in the back; and loss of stature. In middle age, one cannot prevent osteoporosis. All the measures prescribed and described are to prevent *additional* bone loss.

> *In middle age, one cannot prevent osteoporosis. All the measures prescribed and described are to prevent* additional *bone loss.*

There are two components of bone that, if compromised, contribute to osteoporosis: first, the bone density and, second, the structure or architecture of the bony connections and cross-bracings. Although the bone itself is healthy, it is not strong because of loss of integral cross-bracing. To measure density, we currently rely on Dexa bone mineral density (BMD) testing, which measures bone density in two sites: the lumbar spine and the femur (hip) head. It is a relatively simple test, requiring some 17 minutes to perform and requiring nothing more that lying under a scanner.

Thanks to an effective public awareness campaign, most women now know that one in four women in their 50s will suffer from osteoporosis. The likelihood of occurrence is increased if this condition afflicted your mother or grandmother (maybe you remember a grandmother who stooped when she walked or struggled to lift her head?). The cornerstones of prevention are diet and exercise, as well as an assessment of those factors that contribute to increased risk. The awareness of increased risk itself is relevant to how women change behaviors. For example, in a survey conducted by Rubin and colleagues among women who had undergone a bone mineral density test, those who were noted to be at increased risk because of "thin" bones were more likely to take measures to offset their risk of future fracture.[1] How so? For one thing, they were more likely to start hormone replacement. In addition, they were more fearful of falls and were more likely to limit their activity to avoid the risk of falling. All these reactions were a personal response to new information. Also, they received medical advice regarding treatments, calcium supplementation, and exercises, all of which they acted on. These issues will be outlined in greater depth in this chapter. However, it is the individual reaction and strategies that are the foundation of success in the approach to osteoporosis. Such contribution cannot be underestimated.

> *The cornerstones of prevention are diet and exercise, as well as an assessment of those factors that contribute to increased risk.*

BONE DENSITY TESTING

The standards by which to define thin bone and osteoporosis in terms of bone density were set by the World Health Organization (WHO) in 1994 and are based on data provided by postmenopausal Caucasian women. The consensus measure of the WHO is based on the Dexa bone mineral density measurement expressed in a T score, which represents degrees of deviation from young, healthy women. Osteopenia is defined as a T score, a rating obtained by comparing the subject's bone density with that of young healthy women, between minus 1 and minus 2.5. Osteoporosis is defined as a T score below minus 2.5. All clinicians agree that scores below minus 2.5 place people at unacceptable risk for fracture.

While these data may not be directly applicable to the majority of women in the world, two broad outcomes are hoped for. One, that by raising awareness of a potentially disabling condition which takes years to evolve, all populations will be able to share the data and strategies for intervention. Therefore, even if testing and treatment are not readily available, there is heightened awareness about the problem and the benefits of all treatments, and public information campaigns can be co-opted. At the very least, the information is able to provide basic knowledge about bone aging and its hazards. Two, that the information gleaned from these studies will provide the basis of extended testing in other population groups in ways that will illustrate differences, whether they are genetic, racial, or dependent on lifelong dietary factors and circumstances.

Once thin bone or osteoporosis are identified, and depending on the patient's age, any number of treatments can be offered and steps taken to offset further loss in bone density. The BMD test then becomes the tool to assess the benefits of treatment and measure progress. This is done by following the BMD on a yearly basis (it generally takes a year to determine how well the subject has responded to the various treatments).

Bone mineral density testing may be considered a rite of passage for midlife women, but there is currently no advisory to doctors to screen every woman patient in this age group, so some assessment of risk is pertinent. Women may want to consider asking for a BMD test if they answer yes to any of the items in the list below.

When to Request a BMD Test

1. You have a family history of osteoporosis.

2. You have obvious and visible frailty, and low weight.

3. You have persistent and inexplicable back pain.

4. You are menopausal and have questions about the value of starting HRT.

5. You smoke.

6. You use prednisone or steroids over a long period of time.

7. You have a sedentary lifestyle.

MENOPAUSE'S PROMINENT ROLE

While, from the mid-30s on, bone loss is a reality for both men and women, there is one time in a woman's life when bone loss accelerates, namely within the first 5 to 10 years of menopause. The component of the bone in question is that portion which is estrogen sensitive. While the degree of loss varies from woman to woman (which is why your mother's history is so rel-

> *Bone loss accelerates within the first 5 to 10 years of menopause.*

evant), it is generally thought to represent between 5 and 15 percent of the total bone mass. Hence the need to identify those women who may have an accelerated pattern of loss, since there is no doubt that good, architecturally strong bone is easier to maintain than to replace.

The test most commonly given involves a serial recording of the bone density in the lumbar spine (between the ribs and the pelvis) and the hip. The resulting measurements can then be compared over a period of time. If the bone loss is progressive, several options are available to the woman, such as maintaining hormone replacement therapy (HRT) or starting it if menopause has occurred or she is using other drugs to help stop or reduce the loss. Although HRT can be started at any time in life, there are two issues that become problematic for women who choose to start estrogen therapy later in the course of bone loss.

The first issue is that if a woman has been off the hormone for a number of years, restarting can result in uncomfortable breast tenderness. In addition to this troublesome side effect, there is a possibility of having to reinstitute cycle bleeding, which is why so many women on this regime cease to comply with it. The second issue is that if significant bone loss has already taken place prior to starting estrogen therapy, the replacement occurs on a structure that is inherently weaker than it would have been at the start of the process. This is why the emphasis is on early detection.

CAN DIET ALONE PREVENT BONE LOSS?

By "diet" I am referring not only to calcium but to the whole range of nutrients that we ingest, including protein and mineral sources. This has been an area of intense study by many disciplines for more than three decades and, while much is known, the applications for an aging population remain unclear, or at the very least, the results continue to maddeningly provide suggestions for further study. For example, let us look at protein.

The recently published study from the Framingham group's osteoporosis study (see p. 57) showed that those with the lowest reported protein intake also had the greatest bone loss in the spine and femur. Also, much effort has gone into trying to understanding the effects of animal protein as a contributor to the potential high acid-ash diet of the average North American diet and its contribution to the leeching of calcium from bone. This means that even small changes in the body's acidity cause a huge stimulation of osteoclastic (breaking down) activity in bone as it fights to buffer the acid. We also know that the average North American diet provides about 1 meq (millequivalent) acid per day, which requires about 2 meq calcium to act as a "buffer." Further, the recent Dash Diet Study for hypertension has shown that an increase from 3.5 to 9 servings of fruit and vegetables per day can promote bone density while reducing heart disease risk factors.

None of these studies proves that there is only one correct mechanism for maintaining strong bone. Rather, we need to acknowledge that the pathways are interdependent and multileveled.

THE DIAGNOSIS IS OSTEOPOROSIS—WHAT NOW?

To a greater or lesser degree, all the answers to the questions posed and issues raised in this chapter refer to both elderly mom and caregiver daughter. The chances are that if your mother had an atraumatic (not caused by injury or accident), usually a vertebral, fracture any time before she turned 80, your risk for osteoporosis more than doubles from the normal lifetime risk that women are faced with as they turn 50. (Remember the huge role genetics plays in bone health that I told you about at the beginning of this chapter?)

So how do we reduce the likelihood of osteoporosis, both for your mother's sake and your own? Many of the products now in development for the treatment of osteoporosis will, during the next 10 to 20 years, change the face of medical treatments; we expect to see significant improvements.

One of the major roles that is best played by the family or close friends is that of risk assessment. Factors that need to be considered include:

- The patient's potential for falls.

- The need for aids for stability, and risky behaviors in the home, like climbing on chairs.

- Knowledge of patient's habits, e.g., eating, sleeping, alcohol intake, routines, and exercise or activity.

- Medications the patient is taking and their effects on her mental sharpness and mobility.

- Physical hazards in the home, such as loose mats or lack of handles in the bath.

One of the touchiest issues that comes up when dealing with osteoporosis is the use of a cane or a walker. Most elderly patients resist this notion mightily, as they believe it indicates they are frail, dependent, and unstable. So I will often ask a daughter to support me in explaining and promoting the benefits, such as a place to sit when tired, the assurance that feeling weak will not necessarily mean the inability to get up or to walk, and independence. Walkers are expensive but they are now also sexy, multicolored, and ultra-light—and, in Ontario, underwritten by the Ministry of Health's Assisted Devices Program (they may be underwritten by other provincial governments as well). A walker will allow mom to get to the community center for the senior exercise program or to the heated pool for the arthritic exercise class.

Part of ensuring your mother is involved in this level of activity is finding community-based programs that suit her needs. Usually many hours are invested in exploring and initiating these services. Then comes the real work of convincing her both of the value of such activity and that there is available transport. Many communities will provide transport to centers, either as a part of a larger seniors' service or as a part of government public transport services. Other resources may be found through church groups or activity clubs, which may organize specific trips and outings for seniors. Most importantly, accessibility in all these circumstances mean staying local. Endurance is not a given in our elderly population. Becoming too tired not only increases the risk for falls but also becomes a disincentive to getting out of the home.

Encouraging mom to maintain her fitness and strength, and regularly checking that her medications are not causing confused and muddled thinking, will help prevent falls and promote her alertness.

THE ROLE OF VITAMIN D AND CALCIUM

Vitamin D by itself will not prevent bone fractures. However, in 1992, an interesting study found that a daily dose of 1,200 milligrams of calcium taken with 800 international units (IU) of vitamin D reduced the fracture rate of both hip and spine in a

For some midlifers Vitamin D and calcium can slow the loss of bone mass to about 1 percent per year.

population of 70-plus year olds. Therefore, this dosage may be considered an effective antifracture therapy in this older population.

For the younger population of midlife women, vitamin D and calcium are able to slow the loss of bone mass to about 1 percent per year. (However, it will neither stop the loss nor replace the bone.) This percentage, though small, is considered significant, given that postmenopausal bone loss can range from 2 to 5 percent per year. Nonetheless, the combination of calcium and vitamin D is not regarded as a true preventative therapy in the face of osteoporosis—it must be supported with specific medications, such as hormones that retard breakdown or promote rebuilding, and with exercise regimes that specifically target bone remodeling.

Getting Sufficient Calcium in Your Diet

Make no mistake, North Americans are dairy eaters, and most of our common sources of calcium are provided within a heavy loading of dairy products. Most adults, however, often experience an increasing intolerance for dairy products as they age. This often presents itself as abdominal bloating, cramping, diarrhea, fullness, and indigestion after dairy-heavy meals. Once we have identified whether the problem is fat intolerance or milk protein aversion or lactose intolerance, relief is often found by removing dairy products from the diet.

So how does one ensure a daily intake of 1,000 milligrams of calcium from other sources? Usually this question is asked by women who are adverse to simply taking a pill, since that amount of calcium is easily obtained by taking two 500 milligrams extra-strength Tums or a generic calcium carbonate, which can be handily obtained at the pharmacy or the heath store. If you are keen to obtain the dose through dietary means, here is how your diet might look for most days of the week, insuring four servings a day of any of the following.

Food	Calcium (milligrams)
Calcium-fortified orange juice, 250 ml (1 cup)	360 mg
Soy beverage, fortified (So Good), 250 ml (1 cup)	330 mg
Salmon with bones, 1/2 can	225 mg
Sardines with bones, 4	200 mg
Spinach, cooked, 250 ml (1 cup)	258 mg
Collard greens, cooked, 250 ml (1 cup)	357 mg
Tofu. firm, raw, 120 g (4 oz)	260 mg
Blackstrap molasses, 30 ml (2 tbsp)	288 mg
Almonds, 125 ml (1/2 cup)	200 mg

HOW IMPORTANT IS EXERCISE FOR BONE HEALTH?

Exercise is vital for healthy bones and its role cannot be underestimated, even for the frail elderly. This population of patients is the foundation of all our understanding that even modest activity programs were helpful in building strength and helping medications work better. We have come to understand that exercise is site specific; in other words, to build strength in the hips, you must "load" the legs and back through walking rather than, say, swimming,

Exercise training provides the same benefit as calcium and vitamin D in offsetting the 1 percent per year bone loss attributed to aging.

which is essentially an antigravity activity. To strengthen the thoracic (the area between the neck and waist) spine, you must "load" the back through weight-bearing exercises for the arms and upper back.

An exercise program undertaken at menopause will effectively offset the 1 percent per year bone loss in two ways. The activity will ensure endurance and sustainability, and resistance exercises will build strength. The concept evoked is that of "exciting the bone" to remold and hold its density and remain strong. Studies have shown that this kind of exercise training provides the same benefit as calcium and vitamin D in offsetting the 1 percent per year bone loss attributed to aging. Even more important for women diagnosed with osteoporosis, site-specific exercise programs have been found to be beneficial in reducing back pain and therefore the amount of pain medication needed. These women also reported better quality of life as a result and felt they had more balance and thereby a lowered potential for falling.

Starting an Exercise Program Safely

This is an area my patients and I discuss at every physical examination and at every opportunity—not because I want to become a drill sergeant but because, as years pass, needs differ and therefore the opportunity to start certain activities is geared to age and time. For example, I encourage all my women patients to begin walking. A good pair of walking shoes along with the Nike slogan of "Just do it" is often all it takes to start the program. Finding the time—usually the greatest impediment—is possible. For example, you could walk during your lunch hour or you could extend your walk from the bus stop or subway station to give yourself the 30 to 40 minutes needed to feel the benefits of a brisk walk.

My real goal is to persuade my patients that there are no 30 minutes more important in the day than these. Devoting 30 minutes of precious time to their well-being often seems an impossible goal for many of my patients. It is the time-crunch pattern repeating itself anew, and it is insidious. My patients are not intractable couch potatoes. They simply view this 30 minutes as a luxury for which they cannot spare the time. Once they start, though, most do not need my encouragement to continue the activity. They feel the benefits in terms of increased endurance and abdominal strength, and they begin to value the island of solitary time.

Eventually, I will encourage participation in classes, be they exercise, step, yoga, or dance. I do this based on my interviews with several trainers who address the specific needs of women in exercise. These trainers commented that women will seek out, and benefit from, the social rather than the competitive context of exercise. They also noted that certain women are calorie-conscious and so food for them will never be simply an issue of fuel for energy—it will also be an issue of appearance and weight.

Hormones will always affect performance, so there is a need to allow for variability. Premenstrual states drain many women's performance capacity, and women need coaching to allow for the drag and often the inertia that saps resolve and motivation. And women are more likely to answer to an internal motivator as opposed to an external challenge or drive. It is not an external push to compete so much as inner drive to change oneself, to answer self-propelled needs or desires for change, that motivates women.

The trainers also note that since women have weaker muscles than men, any program designed for women must have exercises that will enhance endurance and increase strength along with flexibility. The programs should include push-ups, pull-ups, crunches, lunges, and back extensions. Consequently, programs that accommodate these factors are likely to be well received, and women will thrive within them.

Of particular interest with regard to back erectile strength is a specialized exercise program for women with kyphosis (curvature of the thoracic spine related to osteoporosis). This exercise resulted after only three months in an increase in back extensor muscle strength and a decrease in the thoracic curvature. There is indeed hope for your stooping mother.

Having said all this about exercise for the elderly, it may still be equally applied to midlife women. In fact, the mantra for all these women might be better "push up, pull up, crunch, lunge, and extend" instead of "just do it." As a way of empowering women, there is little we can do that is as effective as feeling the core of strength from a tuned body. And there is little that can be a better foundation to carry into our 60s and 70s and 80s and ...

5

KEEPING A BREAST
OF THE SITUATION

Breast as transitive verb: Inflected forms: breast·ed,
breast·ing, breasts. 1. To rise over; climb: "He breasted a rise
and looked down. He was at the head of a small valley"
(Ken Follett). 2. To encounter or advance against resolutely;
confront boldly. 3. To push against with or as if with
the breast.

AMERICAN HERITAGE DICTIONARY OF THE ENGLISH LANGUAGE

In a way, the relationship that women have with their breasts after age 50 is perverse. I'm comparing it with the first blush of pride that women radiate when they bring their daughters in for the "big examination." Not the sex education visit but the one that precedes it, the one in which I ask if the periods are manageable because the evidence of young womanhood (and indeed she radiates youthful vibrancy) signals that all is in place within a taut, newly curvaceous frame.

That innocence is all too soon replaced with concern, if not obsession, with attracting the right attention from admiring eyes. We know the scene—it's heard by mothers everywhere—I'm too small or too big or (God help me) lopsided. Manufacturers and advertisers alike have sniffed opportunity in this and have answered the call with push-ups, fill-ins, or flatteners as the prevailing fashion may dictate. The goal is clear: Breasts are the way to attract the means to fulfill your destiny. Taut, pert, or voluptuous, they are part of the armamentarium. If you read any of the men's and most of the women's fashion magazines, breasts are what define femininity. Time passes, and sexual appeal, more or less defined by those two midchest items, eventually gives way to a mother's breasts as the source of all contentment, satisfaction, nurture, warmth, and safety.

By the time you are ensconced in your 40s, your children may comment that your boobs hang a bit low, and certainly many a patient has managed that sag with a trim and an uplift. Often, these women will opt for "less is more" and are happy to report the pleasure they feel when they lie down in bed and don't find their breasts lying beside them on the mattress. For many, such pertness was not even appreciated in those far-off days of yesteryear, when their breasts did stand on their own even when *they* were lying down.

So how is it that by middle age breasts are something to be wary of, as though they may have some insidious intent on waylaying the unsuspecting? How come we now have to address the issues of illness, tough drugs, fear, and death around this physical touchstone of what has been perceived as the fountain of womanhood? And this is the new reality in a nutshell—from the years of warding off young enthusiasts from copping a feel through and past the years of tiny kneading fists, women now enter the phase of becoming their own cops required to pat themselves up in the furtive search for trouble.

In truth, I often suggest to my patients that one of the many good things about turning 50 is that if they have done so without receiving the dreaded breast cancer diagnosis, they have indeed reached a milestone. This does not in any way mean that the need for diligence is over. However, a lot of anxiety on the part of the doctor and the woman about the anticipated course of a breast cancer has been wrested away from the premenopausal state. This is because, of the 19,000 new cases of breast cancer reported in Canada every year, 78 percent of which occur in women over 50. And while the mortality rate from breast cancer reported from 1986 to 1996 is decreasing, the incidence of the disease is increasing.

Having said this, do I treat the questions that women raise in the office any differently? Are the questions different for women in their 40s than they are for women in their 60s? By and large no. The questions that women want answers to are the same no matter what their age, and although the approaches are somewhat influenced by a woman's status pre- or post-menopausal, the guidelines are universal. Consequently, this chapter is about breast

> *The lifetime risk of developing breast cancer in a 50-year-old woman is one in 18; for a 75-year-old woman it is one in 13.*

cancer and about advocacy and even more about the wealth of information that is now available to women, their families, and friends about this disease and how to cope with it. Indeed, of all the chapters in this book, this one is most dedicated to ensuring that you have access to good Internet sources, and if you do not, that good support for answering your concerns can be achieved. That is the road to a rich maturity.

I'VE FOUND A LUMP

Women felt misled, even betrayed, by the medical profession about a practice that for 30 years has been a part of the lexicon of breast cancer early detection, if not prevention.

For 30 years we have been teaching women how to do breast self-examinations. We know that some diagnostic tools are superb and others are shaky. Breast self-examination has always been shaky and has been under scrutiny as long as it has been in existence.

One evening, I found myself on a subway in rush-hour, squashed in an upright position, my medical journal open in my hands and the title of the article in plain view: "Should women be routinely taught breast self-examination to screen for breast cancer?"

"Oh, you have the article! Where did you get it? It's just been on the news and you have the article!" The voice came behind my shoulder, and I turned to see the face of a woman I didn't know. I acknowledged that the article had been published in the *Canadian Medical Association Journal* and turned the cover over for her to see. How odd, I thought, that our common ground was first a media announcement, as though the published journal article were a mere afterthought. But the stranger was already in full tilt with her dismay at the article's findings, namely that breast self-examination was a useless exercise. She voiced her dismay to another woman who stood facing us in equally close confines. And that prompted a story of a breast lump, found by this third woman, that she probably wouldn't have registered if it weren't for self-examination.

We rode only three subway stops together, but in that time a lively conversation had ensued as heated commentary was exchanged between these women. Mostly they were indignant that someone would suggest that the edict they had held as gospel for so many years could now be tossed aside as a useless exercise and of no value whatsoever. Their reaction reflected what had been happening all day in my office—it had been one of those days that is eaten up with trying to explain away seemingly bad news, when headlines have been only skimmed on the way into the office but you know there will be enormous fallout.

"If I had counted on the mammogram only, they would have missed the cancer totally," said one of my patients, arriving for her physical exam with newspaper in tow. "The nurse even called me to say that all was well and the mammogram had reported no lesion. It was only when the lump persisted and the surgeon eventually was persuaded to insert a needle and withdraw the fluid that they found the malignant cells. Where would I have been if I hadn't found the lump and then been both-ered enough by it to pursue it in spite of the 'normal' mammogram?" We agreed that the practice of medicine is an inexact art and we are, at times, blessed with both the good luck and good sense to demand some action in the face of persistent doubt. While "listen to your body" is often the clarion call of physicians to their patients, it is not exactly scientific.

> *The probability of a woman dying from her breast cancer by age 54 is 1 in 136 and by age 75 it is 1 in 39. This reflects the length of time women will live with the disease, not the incidence per se.*

The heat generated by the media coverage of the study was from women feeling misled, even betrayed, by the medical profession about a practice that has become a part of every woman's yearly self-care and which for 30 years has been a part of the lexicon of breast can-cer early detection, if not prevention. Does it help to say as a physician, "Oh, we've had this information for years"? Tread carefully here or the issue does indeed become a Watergate of breast cancer detection and prevention: What did you know? And when did you know it?

So let's talk about what we know from this study, acknowledging that as studies go, this one is pretty good. With the clarity and single-mindedness that only a fledgling surgeon can bring to the task, asking why do we do this and where is the evidence for it being a useful maneuver, the young doctor who authored the study methodically searched the medical literature. In the repertoire of breast surveillance, there are presently only three maneuvers: breast self-exam, clinical examination by a professional, and mammography with or without ultrasound.

The study addresses the criteria to which all doctors wish to adhere and be guided by when caring for their women patients. That standard is called "evidence based medicine," and it means that what guides our practice in this instance is based on the evidence gleaned from careful and thorough studies and not dogma or tradition. The study utilized the latest means to review large studies worldwide; it had evaluative tools built in to ensure the quality of these studies; it expanded on, updated, and reviewed ongoing studies that have been previously reported. Also, it made reference to the 1994 study from the Canadian Taskforce on Periodic Examination, which advised that the evidence to include instruction on breast self-examination as a part of a woman's yearly physical as a tool for breast cancer screening was not very good.

As all doctors know, based on that study's recommendations, breast self-examination warranted a C rating in 1994; in other words, it was inconclusive whether the practice of breast self-examination was beneficial or harmful: it was neither helpful nor injurious as far as scientists could tell. Nevertheless, physicians continued both to encourage patients in doing breast self-examinations and to provide instruction so their patients could feel competent in carrying out this procedure. Did any physician spend a lot of time advising that this may be useless or even harmful? Not on your life. Doctors don't say, "I'm going to teach you to examine your breasts but doing this examination won't necessarily save your life if you get breast cancer." Nor do we say, "I'm going to teach you to examine your breasts so you can scare yourself silly and have a lot of unnecessary procedures done to you." What we are trying to do is provide a means of enabling women to monitor changes in their own breasts and to seek advice in a timely fashion if they are concerned with any change they may find.

Doctors are concerned with early detection to assure *longevity*, they look beyond mortality statistics, and they must deal with the anxiety generated when a lump is found. Whether the lump is found by my patient or an attentive lover or the breast examiner in the clinic, it requires careful examination and a framework of thinking and action that is directed at understanding its presence. Which bring us to the basic tools of the trade: time (often the first and most effective tool), ultrasound, mammogram, and biopsy. What is selected as the means to explain the nature of the lump depends partly on the patient's history and partly on the examination. Essential to the plan is the reassurance that the problem has been addressed adequately. If a patient remains worried that the lump is persisting or changing, in spite of a biopsy or an otherwise reassuring mammogram or an ultrasound, its removal must be considered. Unnecessary procedures, undue anxiety, no real benefit in outcome—these are the criticisms of the breast self-examination naysayers. Women, though, know themselves better than this, and they want the power that is realized in finding a problem sooner rather than later.

At the end of this chapter I have laid out some guidelines as to what constitutes—from a physician's perspective—a good study. These guidelines will enable readers to evaluate and navigate the media minefield of sound bytes.

THE GAIL MODEL

The Gail model was developed by M.H. Gail and colleagues at the National Cancer Institute and is widely used to quantify a woman's risk of developing breast cancer, usually for clinical counseling purposes or to determine a woman's eligibility for clinical trials. In addition, this model allows one to estimate the likelihood that a woman of a given age with certain risk factors will develop breast cancer over a specified time interval. The model—

- is based on data from the Breast Cancer Detection and Demonstration Project, a mammography screening project involving over 280,000 women that was conducted between 1973 and 1980[1];

- was developed by looking at a number of potential risk factors for breast cancer;

- uses five significant predictors of a woman's lifetime breast cancer risk:
  1. current age
  2. age at menarche (first menstrual period)
  3. number of breast biopsies
  4. age at first live birth
  5. number of first-degree relatives with breast cancer

How Does the Gail Model Calculate Risk?

To use the model, the five pieces of information listed above must be known. The easiest way to use the Gail model is through an interactive computer program, which asks the user to enter the necessary information and then immediately calculates the patient's cumulative breast cancer risk over the next 10, 20, and 30 years. The program, intended primarily for health-professional use, is available online as a breast cancer risk assessment tool at the National Cancer Institute's website. A hand-held version of the model has been packaged for physician use in calculating the risk as they sit with individual patients.

What Does the Gail Model Tell Me?

Cumulative risks of breast cancer calculated by the Gail model may be used in a clinical setting to provide individualized information to women about their breast cancer risk. Using the Gail model, clinicians may—

- identify women who are at increased risk;

- discuss modified options for breast cancer screening, such as beginning mammography at a younger age or having more frequent clinical breast examinations;

- provide reassurance to many women who had previously overestimated their risk of breast cancer.

If the clinician doesn't have the special hand-held computer to calculate the risk, knowing the patient's family history is a more than reasonable substitute. Most women know if they are at high risk.

THE MAMMOGRAM IS SUSPICIOUS—WHAT'S NEXT?

One of my patients, on turning 50, had decided to mark the event by having her first mammogram. It was reported as suspicious and she was referred to my office for further investigation. Clearly, she was beside herself with worry as I undertook to examine the suspect breast and then affirmed that the two nugget-like masses indeed needed to be removed. I began immediately to set out a strategy to guide her through the process of diagnosis and treatment. Already we knew that this was most likely not going to be good news. Even though the majority of breast lumps found turn out to be mere nuisances, the anticipation of ominous news overrides all other considerations until the job of diagnosis is done. Sometimes, you just know.

I am not sure that had events been the other way around, that is, if she had come in for an examination before the mammogram, I would have behaved differently. For mammograms are not innocuous. In one 10-year study in which the mean number of mammograms was four, 24 percent of women were recalled for false positive results. Since this generates anxiety, it is important to appreciate the wait time to the investigation of false positive mammograms. In another study, it was found that the wait time for biopsies for almost half the women was three weeks or longer.

> *Mammograms are not innocuous. In one 10-year study in which the mean number of mammograms was four, 24 percent of women were recalled for positive results.*

I think if I had the advantage of feeling those masses first, I might have chosen to refer her to one of a number of breast clinics within our hospitals that provide a team approach right from the start, so that she would have a little more cushion, a little more support. But many women don't have the option of seeking multiple opinions from clinicians in big teaching hospitals. Some would argue that this saves patients from doing the rounds of doctoring and cross-referrals that, in the search for the best treatment, can plague patients and doctors alike.

There is, however, no quick fix, even with a timely referral. There is the wait for an appointment with and review by a surgeon. There is often a list of other tests to be undertaken, tests having to do with, of all things, the liver and bones—all done to sniff out any indication that the disease has spread beyond the breast. There is the booking of the lumpectomy (the removal of only that portion of the breast containing the lump) and the description of the procedure and perhaps the anticipation of more than an overnight stay. And there is the wait afterward, an endless stretch of time before the diagnosis is handed down. What most women want from their doctor is not necessarily reassurance that it will not be cancer but rather information on what is best for them, their treatment options, and how to ensure they are in a position to obtain them.

DIAGNOSIS CANCER

When a patient of mine is diagnosed with cancer, the first thing I try to do is talk with her along with her partner, a friend, or a family member. Often, I will suggest that they bring in a tape recorder, knowing that they will likely hear only a fraction of the conversation, so terrified or shocked are they by the diagnosis. Many of my patients tell of a state of not really being present for *any* conversation, medical or otherwise, for some time after receiving the news. They exist in a fog of disbelief and fear and surface only as they grapple with the

> *A Canadian study concludes that women will experience better outcomes from breast cancer treatment if they are in centers where they enjoy strong support around their decision making.*

reality of the tough treatments. However, I am not the person who will outline the treatments. What I do for my patient and her family is to set the stage for the procedures she will be going through, and there are many.

First, though, I need to address the urge to cut the lump out quickly and be done with it. Why the wait? Why the delay to surgery? Why can't it be gone tomorrow? And hot on the heels of that urgent issue are the peculiar and specific worries of this particular family.

So it was that I found myself sitting with a patient and her husband after a biopsy had confirmed a malignancy in her. At my request, she brought her husband along, since I had been detecting more anger, in that way that men express their fear, from him than from her. His concerns were many and revolved mainly around the environment as the cause of his wife's trouble. Everything from chemicals to dietary fat but mostly underwiring in bras was on his list as the likely culprit. She sat quietly while he expounded. So I gave him a list of Internet sources he could explore after he and his wife attended to the real issue of how to understand the minefield of staging and treatment they were entering. Then there were their children to consider. How did they see themselves telling the kids? What did they think the reaction would be from each of them? Slowly, as we discussed the girls, we circled back to the husband's fears and his role in how to help his wife through this ordeal.

Sometimes it is not a husband but a senior (in spirit) child that moms will rely on, and often as not it is her most fervent wish that she live to see the kids grown and away or hold the first grandchild. These are the most expressed desires during these sessions in my office. Often I will suggest that the patient and her support person also tape the session with the surgeon after the biopsy information has been gathered together and the real issues of treatment are about to be explained.

Horror stories of dismissive treatment aside, my experience is that doctors, when detailing the best information on the success or otherwise of different treatments, will provide as much information as they feel the patient can possibly endure. Indeed, yet another Canadian study reported recently in the *Canadian Medical Association Journal* concluded that women will experience better outcomes (that is, they'll live longer) from breast cancer treatment if they are in centers where they enjoy strong support around their decision making. In other words, knowledge is power and love is even more.[2]

For many women, the nurse, as part of the treatment team conducting clinical trials such as this study reviewed, may be a tremendous source of empowerment, not only emotionally but also educationally. The nurse will help her patient make sense of all the often conflicting data and how it might fit with that particular patient, regardless of what stage she's reached in her treatment.

A patient once told me that she learned more from the Burlington Breast Cancer Support Group, whose pamphlet she had obtained, than she had learned from me in three years. So impressed was she by the booklet that she volunteered her time to edit the next edition. And so impressed was I by her comment that I immediately called the group up and ordered a gross. It was an information-packed little thing, printed in very small type. But it had it all: staging, treatments, side effects, resources; more than I would ever have thought of or known for that matter. The booklet was the inspiration of the members of that stellar grassroots group begun in 1988 by the indomitable Pat Kelly.

In those days, advocacy groups for breast cancer and breast cancer research were fledgling indeed, and the notion that more is better—by way of information to the patient—was also just barely a glimmer. Now, it is a matter of course to be given a big book about your cancer, and lists and pamphlets and Internet sources by the bagfull. All this is good, and as the information is vital to the decision-making process, more is indeed better.

IS THE CURE WORSE THAN THE DISEASE?

Questions about the safety of the drugs used in the treatment of cancer start when the treatment options are laid out, once all the information that can possibly be assembled about the cancer has been accumulated. Then, the options are presented to the patient. This is done on the basis of an enormous pooling of experience with an abundance of different drugs called, collectively, chemo, with or without radiation, with or without more surgery.

The treatment clinics usually explain the options so well that I'm almost never called upon to render another voice to the strategy of treatment choices. I attribute this to two things. First, to the massive amount of data that has been gathered as a result of combining information internationally on treatment outcomes across thousands of women over time. This means that treatment options are standardized and not done on the whim of any one doctor or clinic. Second, to the rigor of making sure that unified and systematized treatments are applied for that specific tumor so that outcomes can be measured and women can be given clear expectations of how good their chances are with these treatments. Given the range of new agents and the combinations of drugs, without this systematic approach, treatment would be chaotic.

Once on the path we call staging, women find their place in the scheme of things and are clearly helped and expected to make informed choices. These may include all the information on the side effects of specific drugs, the potential hair loss (one family member shaved her head in solidarity with her mother), the nausea, the ulcers, the diarrhea, the falling white blood cell count, the bone-weary tiredness.

Presented with all the options, armed with statistics on outcomes and survival rates, most women step up to the plate and become a part of that information pool for others coming behind them. They do so because now they have a clearer picture of the enemy that has beset them. They have information where before they had only alarm. They have options where before they had only dread. They become a part of the clinical trial data base that both treats them and provides a road map for those who follow. I think this is why I don't see many women back from the clinics: they do their job well.

Not all women will want to explore or inform themselves to the same degree. Some will instead put faith in the information given by the doctors and proceed. Others regard this attitude as fatalistic. To my knowledge, no study has yet been done that finds that one attitude over the other increases mortality.

SUPPORT GROUPS AND ALTERNATIVE TREATMENTS

Treatment of breast cancer involves a lot more than doing the rounds of chemo/radiation clinics or going under the surgeon's knife. Most women will more or less dabble in the alternative or complementary therapies as a part of the quest to gather their strength. I encourage this. I view all such efforts as part of a strategic plan that will find its worth in surprising ways. The first suggestion I make is that women find themselves a support group. I do this early on in the process. Any number of tools may be contained in such groups, and while my patients are assured of getting information, beyond that, there is a wealth of resources available and that others have found useful. They can explore massage, reflexology, reiki, nutrition, healing touch; there are groups for kids, spouses, friends; there are affirmation groups, and question-and-answer groups with leading researchers in the field. There are groups for new starts and recurrences.

I view these groups as both complementary to conventional treatment and the essence of a holistic approach. So, while women may feel like they are standing still in time waiting for their tests and surgery, I present the support groups as a means they can use to help prepare themselves. Such groups are, for many women, a way of understanding and exchanging information on a multitude of topics by hearing the stories of others. Often a patient will tell me of long coffees that another group member has treated her to in order to help my patient make sense of something she's been told. In turn, I am treated to hearing how my patients volunteer their time and energy to the groups or join the hospital's dragon boat rowing team or find some form of activity that has its origins in the group's support.

In time, the chemo treatments do end, radiation stops, and scars heal, but clearly the foundations of inner strength will have just been put into motion.

Out-of-Pocket Options

In addition to the readily available complementary treatments outlined above that are an inherent part of how breast cancer support groups do their good work, patients will invariably explore the out-of-pocket options. These include acupuncture, reflexology, iridology (looking at the colored part of the eye for clues about body states), Chinese medicine, and chi gong, as well as the macrobiotic diets and herbal

> *What matters for women is that they have the financial means to explore aids that will support their basic treatment.*

remedies that purport at the very least to cleanse the body of chemotherapy's toxins and at most to assist the immune system in its defense against the cancer cell.

What matters for women is that they have the means (financial cost is a significant factor in evaluating and opting for these alternatives) to explore aids that will support their basic treatment. By now, most women have begun to emerge from the fog of despair and are ready to tackle the job of cure. Rarely will one of my patients decide to abandon the standard treatments and choose instead to go the whole route with macrobiotics or with a herbalists or some proclaimed "healer," often based in Mexico. Sometimes, they do all this in addition to standard care. Most treating physicians will answer queries about these treatments with a measured, cautious view. After all, most of us have been a part of seeking alternative routes in some formal way since the early 1980s and have been influenced and educated by the work of such pioneers as Dr. Carl Simonton and Dr. Bernie Siegel.

Carl Simonton is a radiation oncologist who, together with his wife, Stephanie Mathews-Simonton, broke new ground with his mind-body techniques for treating cancer and his research in the field of psychosocial oncology. His findings were documented in two books: *Getting Well Again* and *The Healing Journey*. The seeds of his revelations came as a result of treating patients with the tool of his training: X-rays. However, he was perplexed when, despite his best treatment strategies and good expectations for a cure, some of his patients worsened and died. His wife worked in human relations and motivational applications—the power of positive thinking—and it was her suggestion that perhaps there were other motivators preventing cure that launched their idea. Together they created an approach that was patient-centered and called for the mobilization of deeper inner strengths and resources. The results were remarkable. Patients who should have died rallied and in some cases showed no evidence of the original cancer.

Similarly, Dr. Bernie S. Siegel, retired general, pediatric surgeon, author, and former president of the American Holistic Medical Association, has had enormous impact with his holistic approach and belief in the healing potential within each of us. His books, *Love, Medicine and Miracles* and *Peace, Love and Healing*, contain many unusual case studies and explain the foundation of his treatment. He was the first doctor to shave his head so that his bald cancer patients would feel more comfortable talking to him. His pioneering approach of whole person care has expanded the vistas of traditional medicine.

The work of these doctors is now so intrinsic to our treatment philosophy that we do not often acknowledge that its basic value still has a very individual application. Most centers have adopted a variation of this kind of group process as well as the more supportive, informative offerings. These will usually be underwritten by the clinic, the local Cancer Society, or the advocacy group in the area. In other words, they are available in some format that has taken its roots from the masterful awareness of mind-body work.

THE BREAST CANCER WATCH

Breast cancer survivors come by that honorific with their "trial of fire" and "own it" attitudes and with a proud awareness of having surfaced from under the shadow of an experience that will be a part of their lives forever.

With breast cancer remission, you talk of 10 years, then 20 years, then maybe you forget how many "years out" you are. But you never forget how many years out your mother is. Women adopt this vigilance as a part of their lives, initially having appointments every three, then six, months with the surgeon or the oncologist or the radiologist, sometimes alternating between different specialists. Eventually, the appointment becomes an annual event with one doctor, preceded by the usual tests and examinations, a mammogram, blood work, and X-ray. Then, on the appointed day, an examination, a review of body systems, a breast check. Sooner or later, women trust that their own assessment is valid and stop being afraid of what the doctor may find. By that time the appointments have adopted the air of an easy-going chat; the clinicians are trusted, humor breaks through. For a breast cancer survivor, "cure" becomes a nonessential item to live by. Like an abusive relationship, you can walk on from your experience but you are indelibly imprinted by it and, as with most harrowing experiences, the task is to grow through it.

I often liken cancer to two five-pound weights shackled around my patient's ankles. It may not seem a great burden initially, but after a few

> *70 percent of women treated for breast cancer are alive 10 years later.*

miles, it is a real drag. Eventually though, the legs toughen and muscle is formed. Everything becomes clearer, more defined, edges appear, there is strength to carry on. The weights become a part of the leg that defines you.

PREVENTING BREAST CANCER?

So what can you do to prevent breast cancer in the first place? The simple truth is that we don't yet know how to prevent breast cancer. We are very new to this question and various studies are underway. Current medical practice is not traditionally about preventing cancer but battling it. But in the areas of diet, drugs, and genetics, important work is being pursued.

Dietary Fat

There has been a long ongoing Canadian study on dietary fats—the Canadian Diet and Breast Cancer Prevention Study Group—which many of my patients who were deemed at increased risk, because of dense breast tissue on mammography, signed on for. In this study, the study group aims for 20 percent dietary fat; the control group makes daily records of the usual intake of fat in their daily diet.

The typical North American diet consists of a whopping 35 percent fat, and we know that the typical 40-year-old Canadian woman struggles to hold her daily dietary fats to approximately 25 percent. More information on dietary fats are outlined in the chapter on hearts. When the dietary differences between countries and populations of women and breast cancer incidence are compared, it is evident that the lines blur considerably, that populations may not share all that much common ground. The study continues to report.

Drugs

The big new movement in preventative treatment is chemoprevention— actually using medications to reduce the incidence of breast cancer—and it is not without controversy. In 1998, the findings of a study in the prevention of breast cancer in high-risk women mounted by the NSABBP (the National Surgical Adjuvant Breast and Bowel Project, an international cooperative of more than 500 treatment centers with 40 years' experience in conducting trials of treatment and prevention) was reported. Involving some 13,000 enrollees, the study showed that Tamoxifen reduced the chance of developing invasive breast cancer by almost 50 percent in high-risk pre- and postmenopausal women.

The drug is not without some of its own risks, and so now Tamoxifen and its cousin Raloxifene are the subjects of an even bigger study, the Star Trial. This new study seeks to enroll 22,000 postmenopausal women, from all races and walks of life, who must have the risk of a 60-year-old woman to enter. The study will enroll for a period of five years to obtain the critical numbers needed and will run for a five-year period for each enrollee. The reporting is expected to go on for years, as women have agreed to be followed on a clinical basis thereafter. While this is the first study of its kind, it will surely not be the last.

In the future, women may expect that such trials will be commonplace. They may also expect that as new products come into the marketplace, old ones will be replaced. In addition, they may expect that with the regulation (namely, that the ingredients be precisely quantified and identified) of a number of "natural" drug products, more studies will be mounted to affirm the claims being made. The best studies will always be randomized (whether eligible candidates are treated or not is determined by allotment) and "blinded" (candidates don't know if they are on the drug or not). They also will involve enough candidates to show true relevance ("power").

Hormone Replacement Therapy (HRT)

One of my patients saw a breast surgeon about a suspicious lump. When she returned for an office visit a few days later, she was floridly menopausal, as the physician had told her to immediately stop taking her birth control pill. She was 52 and I had started her on birth control a year or two earlier in order to manage irregular periods and her tendency to get ovarian cysts. Even though I knew the mammogram was confirming a likely malignant tumor, I felt that leaving my patient on hormones was justified given that the medical literature supported such a plan on an individual basis.

"Not so," said the surgeon when I called in a huff to object to such a sudden stoppage. "It's just common sense, Jean," she said. There was no waiting to see what the receptor sensitivity was to estrogen or progesterone. Nor was there an allowance that at age 52, suddenly stopping hormonal therapy was bound to create problems. It was full stop upon my patient's leaving the surgeon's office. And while *I* may have been perturbed at the finality of the move, it is no wonder that women are confused and feel let down by the doctors who pronounce that there is no link to breast cancer when they put women on hormonal therapy. "If so," they ask, "why stop this therapy so dramatically and abruptly?"

Why is all hormonal cancer therapy in its essence anti-estrogen? For a long time, the medical profession reported that hormone therapy was in no way linked to an increased breast cancer risk. Indeed, even today doctors are prepared to present a wealth of data that refutes this observation. The data can be fur-

> *Although the physician in me knew that heart disease rather than breast cancer was still the leading killer of women, the statistics held no comfort for me.*
>
> *—Toronto physician Dr. M. Paulson*

ther diluted by talking about a woman's heart disease risk being the greater concern and risk than her breast cancer risk. (It is true that breast cancer in a woman 70 years old or older is not likely to be a killing event, as opposed to heart disease at the same age.) As though women truly equated the two events. But as more and larger population-based studies are reported, such as the Nurses' Study, the link between duration of hormone replacement therapy and increased risk of breast cancer becomes clear and is undisputed.

The Nurses' Study began in 1976 under Dr. F. Speizer, with funding from the National Institutes of Health in the United States, and enrolled 122,000 female nurses, who responded to a written questionnaire every two years. It is now in its 25th year of reporting. For the Nurses' Study, the critical timeline of safety for hormone use was 10 years. After that, the incidence of breast cancer begins to rise. And, since the reporting of the HERS (heart and estrogen/progestin replacement study) in 1998, which refuted the protective benefits of hormone replacement in women with established heart disease as well, estrogen has been decked yet again.

THE ROLE OF HEREDITY AND GENE MARKERS

Often, women will come to see me with a lot of anxiety about their own breast cancer risk because their mother or their aunt has been diagnosed with the disease. In truth, even with this family pattern, the actual incidence of my patient developing breast cancer in this situation is only about 15 percent. However, there are families in which many members have had breast or ovarian cancer, and a relative or two with colorectal cancer. Such a group constitutes a high-risk family, and it is this family that geneticists seek. In addition to counseling all the family members on strategies for prevention, geneticists want to test for a marker gene that identifies the higher risk. Once again, providing information on what constitutes risk and directing families to more information is the job of the discerning family physician.

WHAT CONSTITUTES A GOOD STUDY?

Doctors use a number of criterion to evaluate how good a study is and how important it may be to their practice. If we look at the big drug trials that have influenced how we treat a particular cancer, we are looking at outcomes, the most critical being mortality or, at the least, time to recurrence of the disease. In these studies there is a common element: the cancer. And the more data compiled about it, the better will be the cataloguing of results of treatment. This information is then applied to the next patient and the next;

through this process all treatments can be refined or replaced as newer agents come along. It is a ceaseless battle.

The basis of most treatment protocols used in breast cancer treatment spring from the NSABBP (National Surgical Adjuvant Breast and Bowel Project), which since 1957 has been at the core of all research in America around breast and bowel cancer. The other studies referred to in this chapter (and in the chapters on the heart and bones) are population studies, which are by nature more difficult to evaluate. Clearly these studies have stood the test of time and, as they continue to report their data, their names are touchstones for all women. Framingham (see p. 55), the Nurses' Study, the Women's Health Initiative, the Star trial—all should be recognized as being of value to midlife women. Here's why.

The number of people surveyed is important, since the larger the number, the more likely it is that the study will be able to indicate the differences in treatments or outcomes, thereby establishing their value. This is referred to as the power of a study to show differences that are meaningful if treatments or strategies are undertaken within a group.

Peer review is the means by which clinicians acknowledge that a study poses a question or a proposition and then devises the means to answer it with rigor and acceptable statistical tools.

The Cochrane Data Base is a data base designed to help doctors access such peer-reviewed data and sets high standards for the critical review of a large number of published studies. While the ideal trial is the randomized controlled trial (RCT), most data comes from the big population studies that are subjected to analysis of their many factors. Even with such resources at our disposal, the number of studies now being reported is so great that the estimates of time required to review published data is way beyond the means of most busy doctors. And to compound this issue, since medical journals now have agreements with the media on "breaking" news (claimed to help everybody), many patients arrive with study data even before the hardpressed physician has had time to digest the information.

The information in this chapter reflects the concerns and questions of many of my midlife patients. There are numerous and excellent books on the subject of breast cancer and its treatments—both allopathic and alternative. For those women with breast cancer or those who want more information about the process and studies, I have supplied the addresses of some excellent websites at the end of this book. All this information is and will continue to be useful, if not essential, to us and to our daughters. Please pass it on.

Why take one of the hundreds of stories I hear in the office and offer it as one of the book's few identified-patient narratives? Partly, I think, because Esther is such a public figure who has used her foundation of rich experience to help women understand their bodies. Partly because her story is much like that of all women—multilayered, transformative, and burnished by tribulations that she has overcome in her unique way. Partly because she has positioned herself as a beacon for women who must endure a trial, shift their priorities, and develop new means to cope with illness. Her goal is to help them find their core by continuing to evolve her own. Lastly, because she agreed to be identified after I called her and confessed that I was acting on some imperative that was not of my own making, a mission that was not within my character but seemed necessary in order to tell a story, as yet untold. Thankfully, she agreed, and what transpired was most assuredly a gift for women.

LET IT BREAK YOU OPEN

Does adversity break you open in order to remold your character? Is it necessary to be or to feel broken open in order to go through fires of change that take you to another place or forge a different being? Why and for whom are we here? All these questions emanate from the small form of Esther Myers.

You do not know you are in the presence of a true radical when you meet with her. The colors in her home are warm and vivid; baskets full of brightly colored wool line the walls, and sand dollars, shells, feathers, and paper from a wasp's nest sit on the shelves. She moves with fluidity and grace, making no sound; her speech is soft and her gaze intense. When I speak she soaks up my words; when she replies, it is with all the care her experience and expertise affords. Nonetheless, she is a radical and has probably always been so—not aggressive or militant in a radical militaristic, anarchistic sense but in the real sense of "going to the root" of issues.

Born the eldest of four children, Esther's upbringing was liberal Jewish and the household became kosher after she herself was sensitized by going to Hebrew school. Her young life was touched by her mother's roller-coaster bouts of mental illness, and she remembers a series of severe episodes while in high school.

The family configuration was professional and medical. Her father was an ophthalmologist, many relatives were medically trained. Her sister became a physician and her brother a biomedical engineer. Esther began university headed for a career in chemistry but switched to philosophy, looking for reflection, meaning, and purpose, though it was not to be found in her coursework. Her first radical decision was to not enter graduate school.

Instead, she went to England for one summer and stayed seven years. While there, she engaged in two life-altering events, neither of which related to her first job as a social worker for the Jewish Blind Society. The first one was to live for a time in the "asylums," those group homes initiated by R.D. Laing where the distinctions between therapist-patient roles were purposefully blurred, and where the process of a breakdown was seen as a breakthrough rather than as mental illness or schizophrenia. It was while living as part of that community that the second occurred. A free class in Iyengar yoga was offered to the residents of the asylums. Esther took to the practice like "a duck to water."

When Esther returned to Canada in 1976 at age 29, her family was in crisis. Her mother was dying with breast cancer and her father's post was threatened by a movement to close the hospital where he worked. Gradually, she resettled and started to teach yoga. From the very beginning she was a teacher of teachers. In 1979, she opened her own studio in Toronto's Annex. The studio has become an establishment in the community, well known and utilized.

Iyengar yoga, which Esther introduced to Toronto, and karate in which she holds a black belt, have been the vehicles with which she has accessed and engaged those parts of herself that are assertive, fierce, strong, and independent. Positions, in particular the warrior poses, which are the foundation of Iyengar yoga, can represent standing on one's own two feet, taking a stand, standing up for one's self, knowing where one stands. To have even momentary glimpses of herself as a powerful warrior took quite a few years of practice.

In 1984, when she was already a leading teacher in Toronto, Esther came under the instruction of a remarkable 78-year-old Italian teacher, Vanda Scaravelli, author of *Awakening the Spine*. For the next 10 years, Scaravelli spent the summer and fall in Toronto. Under her remarkable tutelage, Esther thrived and blossomed.

In 1994, Esther was diagnosed with breast cancer and her life's work broadened.

For me, the first truly different thing that happened was telling my students that I was going for a biopsy—and I still don't know why I did that. It was such a break from my usual teacher-student relationship. My sense of privacy had always prevented me from so publicly exposing myself as someone who was scared, endangered, vulnerable, weak. That declaration opened a channel for the extraordinary support that flowed for months.

In addition to the unconditional support of family, friends, colleagues, and students, having a family full of doctors and researchers meant I had access to complete and accurate medical information, delivered with care and compassion. I was surprised at how hard it was to consciously open myself up to accept all the love and caring being sent in my direction.

When I went in for the biopsy, I didn't think the "suspicious" areas that had shown up on a mammogram would be cancerous. When I got the diagnosis, it fractured me in two ways. One was the diagnosis itself, the other was that in spite of all my years of training and body work and lifestyle, all my "knowing," I had been wrong. Now, I had no faith in my own intuition about what I knew of my body.

The mastectomy that followed was the beginning of a huge healing process because it took my yoga practice to a place it had never been. I had no experience of not being able to stretch and move easily, and I was forced to practice what I preached—"take time, breathe, unwind, let go." Then, five years later, I had a hysterectomy for removal of an ovarian tumor, and I remember thinking, at least I know how to do this. Even now, every time I move in my yoga practice or teaching, the ever-present scar tissue is in my face, reminding me that I have had cancer twice. I know that while I do everything I can to promote healing, my life is not in my own hands.

What is the effect on my sense of myself as a woman? There are a couple of levels to this. I was well through menopause before either of the surgeries. I stopped having periods by age 45, two years before my breast cancer diagnosis. But each surgery left me somehow less—less uterus, less ovaries, less a breast. My feelings about myself as a woman were unbalanced, and my feelings about sexuality and femininity were now even more tied into my yoga work and Vanda's teaching. Her view was that this work was very organic, sensual, orgasmic even. So I have had to address my own sexuality and womanhood in my practice of yoga.

The diagnosis of breast cancer also opened up a psycho-spiritual crisis. At first, I gave myself two years, saying, you have cancer and you're going to die. There was no medical basis whatsoever to this notion—it was purely my terror of dying. Two years to achieve my life's goals, I thought. I wanted to do two things. One was to make my relationship with my partner better, and the other was to continue to teach. Teaching helped me carry on being myself, between visits to doctors, alternative healers, and therapists. In the first few months after the surgery, teaching one hour of simple breathing and relaxation left me too tired to manage the 15-minute walk home. The exhaustion was a lesson in priorities. With very limited energy, I became an expert in time management, asking myself constantly: "Is this what I really want to be doing?" "Is what I'm doing right now really important?"

The other area that opened for me had to do with my feelings about myself as a woman and my sexuality. At the time of my mother's death, she had no breasts and no uterus. I was haunted by this image. When I was faced with the decision to have a mastectomy, the image of disembodied breasts rose like a specter. I was deeply grateful when my father said that my mother was no less a woman because of it—this affirmation gave me unbidden relief. His other great gift came when he said that it was a testament to the strength of genetic predisposition that in spite of everything I had done, this had still happened. It freed me of the New Age Guilt Trip—that somehow my unorthodox lifestyle hadn't prevented this.

In 1996, I began teaching yoga classes for breast cancer patients at the newly opened Marvelle Koffler Breast Centre in Mount Sinai Hospital, in Toronto. I was excited at the opportunity to teach yoga in a hospital setting, and I wanted to give something back. I found that most women came to classes toward the end of or after their medical treatment, when they had the time and the psychic energy. Yoga is also seen as one way to continue participating in one's healing, when medical treatment has stopped. For some, yoga was seen as a crisis intervention, a way of helping themselves to get on with life again; others have continued for years. The classes function in a supportive and caring environment. The supportive aspect came out of my understanding of where women were at in the course of their therapy and how they were feeling, which enabled me to adapt the classes to their needs.

My experience with cancer survivors has highlighted women's need for self-care and empowerment. In my beginners' classes, I often emphasize that this is time for "you." Since so many women have been conditioned to ignore or deny themselves in favor of others, it can be a real struggle for them to honor their own needs and to value themselves and their feelings. It seems to me that much of my work both within myself and as a teacher is in building ego: empowerment, feelings of self-worth and self-esteem, competence, power, authority, authenticity.

In 1998, I got a call from a woman in New York state asking if I knew of a yoga practice video for breast cancer survivors. I didn't, but thought it was a wonderful idea. The tape that we made, *Gentle Yoga for Breast Cancer Survivors*, was developed in conjunction with the women themselves brainstorming around what they thought was needed.

Each diagnosis has pushed me into more and more healing work: psychological, naturopathic, body, and spiritual. I don't want to make breast cancer the center of my life, but it infuses my life and there is a resonance of "I've been through the fire," and people know that. In my meditation I have finally been able to look at the specter of death and not run away. My mantra is now, "Let it break you open." I'm not grateful I had cancer, but it certainly has been an extraordinary teacher.

6

Oh, Did I Forget Memory?

Memory is a wonderfully useful tool, and without it judgement does its work with difficulty; it is entirely lacking in me ... Now, the more I distrust my memory, the more confused it becomes. It serves me better by chance encounter; I have to solicit it nonchalantly. For if I press it, it is stunned; and once it has begun to totter, the more I probe it, the more it gets mixed up and embarrassed. It serves me at its own time, not at mine.

Michel de Montaigne, 1533–1592

Alzheimer's Disease

Alzheimer's disease is a progressive loss of mental ability and function, often accompanied by personality changes and emotional instability, by memory lapses and changes in behavior. A common disorder affecting both men and women, it progresses to include symptoms of confusion, restlessness, inability to plan and carry out activities, and sometimes hallucinations and loss of bladder control. The cause is unknown; there is no cure, with treatment aimed at alleviating the symptoms.

Much like breast cancer and osteoporosis but unlike heart disease, which we know kills us, the thought of becoming addle-brained terrifies midlife women. And with predictions for our increased life expectancy, along with the much larger numbers of people getting there, the attendant figures of rising incidence are not very reassuring. The estimated number of people who meet the diagnostic criteria for Alzheimer's has been put at 8 percent.[1] But there are wide variations in the actual prevalence, depending on how old is old. For the young old, between the ages of 65 and 74, the prevalence is low, at 2.4 percent, while for 85 and older, the rate soars to 34.5 percent. Alzheimer's is also expensive, with health care costs related to dementia accounting for more than 8 percent of the Canada's health budget in 1991.

Betty Freidan, in her book *The Fountain of Age*, was of constant good cheer in reporting that only 5 percent of elderly Americans over 65 are in nursing homes and less than 10 percent will ever be. Somewhere between these numbers lies the real truth, but whatever the difference between the fanciful estimated and the grim truth, the uptake in care provision will be parceled out to midlife women. It is they who make most of the arrangements for the increasing care needs of their parents. If, as Ms. Freidan suggests, less than 10 percent of elders will ever be in nursing homes, it points to the only possible and notable conclusion, one which is discussed in more detail in Chapter 9, namely that family members in the home—daughters—will assume the day-to-day care. And all this extra care will not be accomplished by enlisting home care services or community help; those services simply do not exist in quantity or quality in most thinly stretched community-based organizations. They are as threadbare as the frazzled daughter trying to bring more help into mom's home. If the nation spent 8.5 percent of its health care dollar on care for dementia in 1991, that was surely a pittance compared with the out-of-pocket expense that families will pick up as time goes on.

There is no question that a diagnosis of Alzheimer's is extremely distressing to both the patient and the caring relative, usually an adult child, which is why I repeatedly emphasize the need for advance planning. While research continues, we know little about the cause of this disease, but we do know about the intense emotional pain that is felt by those who have to cope and care. While this pain cannot be avoided, it can be better dealt with if there is an open, ongoing dialogue between parent and child, family and doctor.

> *The* Berger Monitor *estimates there are 4.5 million caregivers in Canada, spending collectively about $100 million a week on the incidental expenses of caregiving.*

So, for women in their middle years, the issues around the aging brain are twofold. First, how to ensure the best of care for our parents before they begin to show evidence of a declining mental capacity, and second, how to avoid, if possible, the occurrence of the same decline in ourselves. The second issue, that of avoidance and prevention, is a good place to start deliberation. For all of us in middle age, it is important both that we know how to live well and that we start planning for the care of our elders.

LIVING LIFE TO THE FULL: THE NUNS' STUDY

The remarkable story of the nuns tells us a lot about and supports earlier data on the aging brain. The full impact of this study was not foreseen by Dr. David Snowdon in 1985 when he first approached the Mother Superior of the school sisters of Notre Dame at Mankato, Minnesota, to enlist her help in persuading the sisters to participate. This ambitious study would be a longitudinal assessment of 678 nuns in the order, aged from 75 to 100 years, and would include ongoing memory-testing observation and detailed analysis of their writings through the years. Further, there was a request to permit an autopsy of their brains after death, a prospect that prompted one of the sisters to exclaim that she wouldn't be needing her brain at that point so it was okay with her.

Ten years later, in April 2001, Dr. Snowdon began reporting in the *Journal of Personality and Social Psychology* and the study is the subject of his book, *Aging with Grace*.

Why nuns? Snowdon thought them ideal for scientific study because their stable, relatively similar lives precluded certain factors that contribute to illness. They do not smoke, hardly drink, and do not experience physical changes related to pregnancy. These teaching sisters are white and eat in convent cafeterias, and most were teachers in Catholic schools. When they entered the order, they represented the best and brightest young women of their generation. As a group of aging women, linked by many similarities, including family (20 percent of the sisters in this teaching order are also biological sisters) the women are ideal in defining boundaries of similarities—an essential element in the study of an aging process that will take many years to evolve.

But the young doctor had to persuade them, and he had to become a part of their lives to conduct the study. There is magic as you hear him talk about his remarkable walk with them through life. As he said in an interview, it was like having "a hundred real mothers who love you." And it is clear he has come to love these women; it is evident in his voice as he talks about their vitality and vigor and their decline. It is evident as he describes what he considers to be the hardest part for him: to witness the process of them losing themselves. And it is evident in how he outlines what his approach has become as such deterioration becomes a reality. Touching, nonverbal communications, respect, treating them as adults always—these are his foundations of communication, and they never waver.

His study comes alive with the information gleaned from his subjects' lives, prior to any manifestation of Alzheimer's or other diseases related to aging. Since Alzheimer's disease takes several decades to develop, and the disease has important effects on every aspect of a person's life, Snowdon believes that the long-term view of its evolution is important in providing clues to how to offset its damage.

For instance, he found that differences in mental capacity showed up in nuns with virtually identical backgrounds and even in those who are biologically related. One of the theses that he has evolved to explain this has to do with the notion of "idea density"—that many thoughts are woven into a small number of words, a trait correlating closely with nuns who seem immune to Alzheimer's. The more ideas that were expressed in the writings or autobiographies of the nuns, the better the correlation of their retention of mental faculties over time. The Nuns' Study also affirms the contention that a positive emotional state in early life may contribute to living both longer and better.

This latter observation is supported in other studies showing that depression increases the risk of cardiovascular disease and that people rated as optimists on personality tests were more likely than pessimists to be alive 30 years later. The researchers conducting the National Institute of Mental Health study of survivors after 30 years were struck not only by the length of survival of the participants to 81 years (almost twice the statistical expectation) but by the quality of their mental edge. The participants showed flexibility of mindset and actions, and greater imaginativeness and organization of ideas than the nonsurvivors.[2]

> *Dr. R. Friedland of Case Western Reserve University, Cleveland, Ohio, affirms from his studies that those with Alzheimer's had been less mentally and physically active outside their jobs as young people.*

In Dr. Snowdon's study, Sister Nicolette, for example, is lively both physically and mentally at 93. What is idea density for her? One sentence from her autobiography, written as a young woman, about entering the order illustrates the richness of her ideas: "After I finished the eighth grade in 1921 I desired to become an aspirant at Mankato but I myself did not have the courage to ask the permission of my parents so Sister Agreda did it in my stead and they readily gave their consent."

Sister Nicolette has two surviving sisters in the order: one over 80 and clear thinking, the other over 90 and not so. A fourth sister died at age 80. By themselves these ages alone are remarkable, far above statistical expectation. But beyond that, the findings raise many questions: What underlies the positive emotions? How much of this is temperament? How much is related to peers, family upbringing, and life events? In attempting to draw conclusions from the Nuns' Study, all these questions now become critical. The data pool is enormous and growing, and the survivors are living long beyond their threescore and ten. In the meantime, a trust has been established to secure the data for future study. Snowdon is the first to admit that the wealth of the nuns' bequest to science is bountiful indeed.

When asked what he thinks the core of the nuns' success and vitality is, Snowdon is clear on three key issues: optimism, the role of spiritual belief, and a sense of community that prevented isolation.

What can we take from all this?

Live well.

Be active.

Keep your mind sharp by acquiring new skills and interests.

Take up new activities.

Read.

Work.

Enjoy life.

Be considerate of others.

Seek companionship.

Argue.

Debate.

Explore.

Laugh.

The work of middle age. You get the picture.

BRAIN DRUGS AS PREVENTION

Estrogen's Latest Banner

Now I come to the issue of drugs, vitamins, and herbal remedies as well as meditation, staying mentally challenged, and new learning.

The latest word on the street is that estrogen is a preserver of mental abilities and memory. Memory does appear to be enhanced by being on estrogen. The major focus of Dr. Barbara Sherwin's work in Montreal has shown that being on estrogen has a positive effect on memory tests. If you look at an electron microscope picture of dendrites—those long strands of electrically charged fibers that transmit the neurochemical charges that we call mental activity—with neurons bathed in estrogen and then at a similar picture of these brain cells not so nourished, you can verify that

> *The development of Alzheimer's is a process that takes years to evolve.*

estrogen appears to be a stimulant for the growth of brain cell dendrites. We assume from this picture that estrogen will protect women from suffering the ravages of Alzheimer's as long as their brain cells are sufficiently bathed in estrogen.

Further, an even more controlled study of estrogen's benefits was conducted in a New York nursing home with a very elderly population of women Alzheimer's patients. The estrogen dose was blinded (that is, it was not known who was taking the drug as opposed to a placebo). There was a significant difference in performance between the two groups, with the group on estrogen performing better.

But perhaps the best trial was one conducted in the reverse mode. A pharmaceutical company had to test in a clinical trial an estrogen-like drug (the designer estrogen Evista). It had to answer the question that had been raised as to whether this particular configuration of the drug would block the estrogen brain pathways, therefore predisposing people to Alzheimer's. Since this was a large drug company, the testing was exhaustive and involved many more tools than simply rote memory. Indeed, some of the tools had been developed by the US military. In all, a total of seven different measures were used to test the designer estrogen against a placebo. And, as expected, no differences were found.

The point here is not the effect of the drug. Rather, it is the solid and equally good results of the control group, that is, those who were not on any drug. Insofar as this testing showed, there are no great benefits to be realized either by being on the designer estrogen or not being on it. The development of Alzheimer's is a process that takes years to evolve, and most of the existing tests for memory are simply not capable of predicting who will or will not benefit by taking a drug, through a number of years, in anticipation of protection.

Donepezil (Aricept)

Much like drugs for osteoporosis and heart disease, drugs for the prevention of Alzheimer's are only in the realm of possible and potential. In other words, very new, very crude, with a long way to go. Which is not to say that we cannot expect great things. There will be whole new classes of drugs that seek to offset or delay the decline in people who manifest mental deterioration. The initial drug marketed for mild to moderate Alzheimer's disease—scores of 10 to 26 on the Mini Mental State Exam (MMSE); I discuss this test in more detail at the end of this chapter—was donepezil (Aricept). The benefits are mixed; some patients showed marked improvement in areas such as alertness and significant improvement in scores on the MMSE. Almost one half will show a delay (6 to 12 months) in progression of their symptoms and some (20 to 30 percent) show no response. Consequently, it is to be expected that many more drugs working in different areas of the brain will eventually be composed in cocktail form.

A Vaccine for Dementia?

New work is being done in this area but the studies are very preliminary, and the road unsure. The idea is that a build-up of protein deposits on brain cells is a factor in the progression of Alzheimer's disease. A vaccine, if it can be developed, will enable the body to resist or reduce these protein deposits, keeping neurons clear and presumably functioning better.

Other Anti-Alzheimer's Remedies

There is some suggestion that vitamin E has a place in the preservation of good brain connections and it is enough to advise that 800 IU (international units) is a useful target for which to aim.

In spite of our hopes for gingko biloba, a herb which for hundreds of years has been associated with the ability to improve memory (see Chapter 2), there are no good studies on its benefits.

One of the benefits reported by Dr. Snowdon from the Nuns' Study evaluated the levels of folic acid in brain tissues on autopsy. Although the work is preliminary, there is some suggestion that folic acid levels were higher in those nuns who avoided the onset of Alzheimer's.

MEASURING THE TASK

I have touched on the need for living wills and power of attorney for care in Chapter 9. Here, I will spell out the issues that you and the family doctor will be addressing, at least initially. Like problems with teens, the family doctor's office is often the first place families seek guidance about what is wrong and what to do.

What Happens in the Office

Doctors refer to the four Ds that can masquerade as Alzheimer's and need to rule them out quickly. They are depression, deafness, drug intoxication, and delirium. Once these are eliminated, we will often use a simply administered office assessment tool called the Mini Mental State Exam (MMSE) also known as the Folstein. It is a test that is scored out of 30. Although it is influenced to a degree on the educational level attained by the patient, it is a good place to start (the test is included at the end of the chapter, though it is not meant to be used at home). The first indicator that suggests using the Folstein is the family's expressed worry that there is deterioration from a previous level of function in one or several areas. As I mentioned earlier, Alzheimer's is a process that often evolves during many years.

Beyond testing, such as with the Folstein, which assesses basic information, there are queries, the answers to which can indicate impairment of judgment and loss of insight, queries about physical states, and medications and their purpose. All these issues are then related to how mom or dad is functioning. The areas of function are specific to the personal aspects of living: eating, dressing, toileting, hygiene, and getting around. These in turn are specific to the instrumental aspects of shopping, housework, banking, cooking, and transportation. If there is a degree of impairment, it will usually require some corroboration from family members—essential information for ensuring the adequate planning of resource allocation and support that allows our elders to remain at home with some independence.

One of my patients who had just returned from Scotland where her father died after a lengthy illness, leaving her 89-year-old mother on her own, described a new initiative in that country designed to help maintain seniors in their homes. Each month, when her mother collects her pension, she has the option of claiming a maintenance stipend of the equivalent of about $60. The money is for her to use at her own discretion for the maintenance of her home—grocery shopping, cleaning, sitter (when her husband was alive). This plan gives the senior the power to designate how the money is spent. In addition, in this small town of 1,300 people, the public health nurse or the geriatric nurse specialist, along with a roving general practitioner, secures almost daily visits. All in this community's efforts to help maintain seniors in their own homes.

In Canada, we lack such a comprehensive vision, and the care needs of the frail elderly are dictated by both their individual resources and those of their families. Certainly that was the experience of Karen Henderson as she stepped up to look after her father. After 10 years in the "trench," she feels more than prepared to offer help and advice to caregivers coming behind her.

Her motto is not "if" but "when." She is a proponent of being prepared. With that in mind she founded Caregiver Network Inc. The service includes a newsletter, individual assessment and support, care planning, and monitoring. The newsletter is published quarterly and addresses the problems and vexing issues of being the caregiver for aging parents. One of her seminars is about caregiver guilt and is entitled, "If Only I Were Bigger, Stronger, Faster, Smarter"—to which we could add inexhaustible and wealthy.

LOOKING AFTER MOM—AND SOMETIMES DAD

Now we turn to the vexing question of how we are to manage the care of parents, relatives, and friends. In my practice it is clear that the bulk of caring falls squarely on the shoulders of the women. Within 20 years, the proportion of the population 65 years and older will be almost 20 percent, or one in five. The estimated cost to employers of having employees juggle work and family issues is estimated at $2.6 billion a year. I suspect that daycare centers will eventually by replaced by elder care centers, where a woman drops off a parent on her way to work and picks her or him up as she heads home. In fact, Edmonton has such a program in place. Called Choice, it provides

> *Within 20 years, the proportion of the population 65 years and older will be almost 20 percent, or one in five.*

workers who come to the home three or four times a week in order to dress and help seniors get to a center, where they spend the day, get a hot meal, socialize, and are then returned home and helped to settle for the night. However, for most, the reality is that frail elderlies are prone to fluctuations in health, which make them sporadic candidates for daycare.

The more usual strategies that I witness involve the children in increasing amounts of time and care arrangements that enable one or both parents to stay at home until a crisis occurs. At which point, the children (daughters usually) fly home, take an extended leave, quit work, move in, or move the parent in, and begin an extended process of putting things in order. In an ideal situation, this process can start long before the crisis happens. However, this type of planning requires a dialogue with parents different from that most adult children are comfortable with, unless help and resources are available to ease the way.

The following stories throw light on a fear of the challenges facing those who are coping with and caring for Alzheimer's patients.

And for the Foreseeable Future ...

One of my patients took early retirement from her government job in order to take a travel agent's training course—the first step to fulfilling her dream of guiding small groups on exclusive trips to England. With upgraded driving license in hand, she and her chum from university were ready to embark on their adventure. However, the deteriorating health of her father was to forestall her plans, and she spent the first year of her "retirement" escorting him to numerous medical appointments; arranging for a succession of visiting nurses and community service workers; creating elaborate methods to document the physical measures of his well-being; and, in general, worrying about the incessant slide of his wellness into what she considered appalling frailty. "Why does he want to sleep so much?" became her lament.

Her crusade to forestall the deterioration and thwart the relentless slide to terminal illness failed. He slipped away peacefully and in a methodically predicable time. His death left her mother all alone and our now much greater concern was for her mental well-being as, for 60 years, she had been a wife and mother and knew only that existence. At first, she seemed to handle the demise of her husband with a certain equanimity—gentle tears, past remembrances retold. Then, and all too suddenly, there was rapid deterioration, more mental than physical. When her daughter took her to the local hospital for assessment of an apparent spell, she disappeared and was eventually found outside the hospital morgue, praying with a corpse—an activity entirely within her realm of functioning as a church deacon.

While at that time her health seemed not too bad, unfortunately the slide accelerated, and her daughter's days became filled with the logistics of routine, getting occasional breaks, documenting the days and stages of her mother's deterioration. We have instituted nursing care twice a week so there is help with the type of physical care that mom resists from a family member but is able to take from a stranger. Family members have rallied to provide respite, and once a week they tend to mom for either an afternoon or morning. Participation in a daily, community outreach program for seniors who are in need of supervised care and social contact has been instituted. How often she will make it to this program is always uncertain. Yet, once there, she becomes one of the most social of beings and is able to sing, play cards and bingo, and dance the old country dances.

Sometimes it frightens her daughter when mom pleads to go home (to her childhood home) and starts a round of inconsolable tears. However, the tears are more manageable than the flailing that often accompanies her increasing agitation. For this reason, we increasingly resort to more drugs; drugs to calm, drugs to ensure the best possible mood, drugs to allow for sleep, and not necessarily is any of this for the mother.

Caring for a demented mother is a full-time job but immensely rewarding for one of my near-60-year-old patients. She maintains that her mother's quality of life has improved immeasurably with the increased attention. Rather than feeling consumed by the work of care, she has been liberated. "I have a life back," she says." I'm taking piano lessons again; I'm not going to let the inadequacy of service from home care get to me. I view it as their loss because they could see what a treat she is and she is better for being with me, for sure. And it's not that hard."

The care agency in question has a different view, of course. It has been steadfast in declining the kind of service requests that the daughter has made, since there are now even bigger problems with managing elimination. This, a result of how well-fed the mother is, through intensive and painstaking feeding by the daughter.

Until the Ship Docks ...

Another of my patients is farther along that same trajectory. Her mother failed rapidly after the death of her husband and the loss of the seeming validation that he had brought to her life. Perhaps she was just old, but many of my patients fear the inexplicable deterioration of their remaining parent when the other dies. Stories of giving up abound, along with those of the rapid successions of death in parents over short periods—a fact of life that is of little comfort to the remaining children. As this deterioration unfolded, my patient became the main caregiver for her mother and she was the first to enlighten me about community outreach day programs that were springing up in areas of the city. Regardless of such resources, I was struck by the paucity of home support to provide her with respite from the often grueling 24/7 required to attain her goal, namely to provide for her mother to allow her to live out her days in familiar surroundings. As the care needs increased, my patient's ability to work even part-time was compromised. Such committed efforts give new meaning to the unacknowledged cost to society of having daughters care for parents at home and on their own. Doing it for others as an employee nets salary and status: doing it for your own nets costs and anonymity.

My patient persisted and was present, though not at her mother's side, when she died. Even at the end, she doubted the wisdom of the plan, but she was supported in her decision from an unusual direction. A retired physician from her church became her stalwart ally in helping to keep her mother in the home at the end, when all good conscience seemed to dictate the assistance of the hospital. Without that assurance, few of us would have been able to hold on, especially as the isolation of caring increased.

These events have encouraged my patient to get out and live her life. She is now in her early 50s and actually qualifies as an elder-hostel trekker. So she has signed on for her own Outward Bound journey and will join a tour hiking through New Zealand. She has been getting herself in shape, breaking in boots, and increasing her endurance. She is now able to devote to herself the same care, diligence, and integrity that she lavished on her mother.

A COMMUNITY OF CARE — URBAN STYLE

We may think it is impossible to reproduce the quality and essence of support exemplified by the convent setting that shelters and cares for the nuns mentioned earlier in this chapter. Many retirement homes and graduated care facilities now provide increasing levels of service, as their elderly residents age and become more frail. Placement in a nursing home once was a grim specter for our parents, one that caused great alarm. That scenario is gradually shifting as, even in the heart of a big impersonal city, the "community" begins to supply some of the essential needs for safety, respect, and contact. One of my patients relayed the following story which underscores the response friends are capable of coordinating in order to look after one of their own. It also speaks to the spontaneous compassion and good-heartedness of a small band of caring neighbors.

Mary, Kitty's long-time friend, is a woman in her 50s who, within the last five or so years, has been ravaged with Alzheimer's. Mary still continues to live on her own, but there is a community of care that has assembled to enfold her coming and going, while she waits it out on the list for secure housing. Every day, the local pharmacy provides her medications, and if she fails to turn up, someone phones her or drop the medications off on his or her way home.

Kitty takes Mary up to the cottage on occasional weekends and the pharmacy prepares sufficient medications for the duration. Both these women love the country. They will watch movies late into the night, though Susan finds the constant retelling of the plot line tiresome. It is difficult to direct Mary, and the endless repetition of what they are doing or where they are going frazzles the steeliest nerves. Kitty tells the story of shoveling the path to the woodpile in the winter and laughingly describes Mary shoveling the snow right back onto the path just as fast.

A woman who was always meticulous in her appearance, Mary now has to be reminded to comb her hair and tend to her makeup. Blessedly, she has gone past the terrible anxiety of not remembering where she was to be and why she was to be there—a period that meant endless phone calls for directions and reminding her why she had gone to that particular destination. Mary seems more at ease now according to Kitty, who could not countenance such a state for herself. Now it is Kitty who feels badly for her short temper and her inability to stretch her tolerance to accommodate Mary's needs. Yet she is a vital part of that community of care without which Mary's safety would be even more endangered, her life more pinched, her living more constrained by strangers.

THE GIFT OF PLANNING AHEAD

One of the most difficult discussions in my office is that of disclosure: how to handle the consequences of voicing the real concerns of failing memory, increasing paranoia, anxiety, forgetfulness, and fluctuating emotions. It is often painful to witness the fear, alarm, and defensive denial that any problem exists. There is a real inclination to play along with the "all's well" stance; to do otherwise is real work and can be very painful and vexatious. So why do it? First, because in the long run it is harder work to keep covering up—not only for the senior but also for the family, who adds fretting, guilt, and caution to interactions with their parents. Second, if there is no disclosure, there is no opportunity to hear the wishes of

> The Canadian Study of Health and Aging *predicts that 750,000 Canadians will have Alzheimer's disease by 2031, directly affecting one family in three.*

our parents: financial matters cannot be secured; care directives cannot be put in place, and power of attorney for care cannot be settled while everyone is still in a position to be heard clearly. The best time for any of these discussions is before there is any loss of capacity. However, if there is even a subtle suggestion of altered function, such variation is a clarion call for the family to act with a comprehensive, well-thought-out plan.

Often family members feel afraid to disclose to their parents their discomfort with dad's driving or mom's inability to describe how she will get to a destination. Frequently, these fears are raised by adult children in the doctor's office because they are apprehensive about exposing their parent's failing capacity elsewhere. They believe that the exposure may render their parents more helpless and dependent. My response is to gently explain the alternative—not only the accident potential but the enormous fear that must grip the parent if she or he does not remember how to get home or is unable to divine why she or he is standing in an unfamiliar location. One of my frail elderly patients who lived alone would invariably be found at the small mall near her home. The clerks and shopkeepers knew her and would dispatch a delivery person or neighbor to see her home. Ensuring safety while we work on alternative solutions that will enable independence is often the real work in the office.

Just as vital and as important as the issue of safety in this expression of care directives is the whole process of *understanding* the wishes of our parents. Such explorations of their wishes is always best done well ahead of any crisis. The challenge of a concept of a living will is that it is based on hypothetical scenarios that may not apply in the moment of decision. For instance, decisions may have to be made about such basic measures as tube feeding when eating by mouth is no longer possible because a stroke has brought paralysis but not death; surgical intervention for serious fractures; intravenous fluids and antibiotics for recurrent aspiration pneumonia; even sophisticated investigations and interventions in acute-care hospitals. All these options that hospital personnel may feel obligated to provide as usual care may run counter to the stated wishes of "no heroics" or "no excessive life-prolonging measures" of a personal care directive.

Personal care binders, developed by caregivers and endorsed by geriatric units in hospitals and long-term care facilities, are helpful in sorting out both short- and long-term care plans. They come with guidelines for personal care directives, power of attorney, wills, and application procedures for long-term care.

Recognizing what the issues will be is both the first step in creating a comprehensive plan and a step in the right direction to find appropriate resources. The process itself is usually a 10-year journey. While the journey can be chaotic and fraught with worry, be assured that it can be managed with the agreement and assent of our parent by looking ahead and planning the right care, all the way to the end.

The Mini Mental Health Exam: The Folstein

I have included The Folstein Exam here (see next page) to demonstrate how, in office practice, an assessment of the "first pass" can be done relatively simply. I must emphasize, however, that this test should not be used at home with parents or anyone else. Even with only a few gaps in memory, most seniors will be anxious about this testing and are likely to respond with outrage and anger if family members undertake to do this themselves. However, it is useful to know the parameters of this most basic tool of assessment and to be reassured how well many of our parents would do on such a test. A full assessment is best undertaken in a center that can provide for very comprehensive and sophisticated tests that measure capacity on several levels and usually over many days.

Most people will score 26/30 or better, but the score is in part dependent on the educational level attained or years of schooling and age. But most importantly, assessment of cognitively impaired patients requires caregiver input.

It is clear that over the next 20 years, there will be an enormous groundswell of services and resources for an aging and vital population. We have more intellectual and financial resources in the middle-aged population that will make up tomorrow's elderly than ever before. How we care for our parents now may be expected to become our own blueprint for the future. At least that is our hope in being able to live life to the full.

The Folstein Exam

Orientation (1 point each)

What is (year) (season) (date or day of the month) (day of the week) (month)?

What is (name of this place) (city/town) (country) (province) (floor of the building we are on)?

Registration (3 points)

Name three common objects (apple, table, penny). Take one second to say each. Ask patient to repeat all three. Give one point for each correct answer. Repeat until learns all three. Maximum of six trials. Record number of trials.

Attention and Calculation

Spell "world" backwards (d-l-r-o-w). Score is 1 point for each letter in the correct order.

Recall

Ask for the three objects repeated above (3 points).

Language

Name a pencil and a watch (2 points).

Repeat "no ifs, ands, or buts" (1 point).

Follow a three-stage command: Take a paper in your right hand, fold in half and put it on the floor (3 points).

Read and do the following:

Close your eyes (1 point)

Write a sentence (1 point)

Draw a clock face showing ten to two (1 point)

Total score   /30

7

THE ROLLER COASTER OF RAISING TEENS

One of the oldest human needs is having someone to wonder where you are when you don't come home at night.

MARGARET MEAD, AMERICAN ANTHROPOLOGIST

If there were a "right" way to rear children, I am sure we would have discovered it by now. Doubtless, we will continue the search for the perfect method of raising our kids to be both useful members of the community and true to themselves. How often do we pray that despite us, our teens will outgrow their adolescent tumult and go on to lead productive lives? So we just have to keep our fingers crossed. After all, all parenting is parenting by hope.

As I mentioned in the first chapter, the majority of child-rearing tasks both in and outside the home still fall to women—a whopping 80 percent. Given that and the fact that most single-parent families are headed by women, often without (or with very little) financial or emotional support from the child's father, midlife women dump the inevitable rock and roll of teenage angst into their already overflowing hamper of job, parents, menopause, personal health or lack thereof.

In my role as family doctor, it is most often the mothers who come to me with concerns of what to do, where to go, how to help their teens. Though fathers are not always unaware of the issues, it is women who will use the physician as the first, and often last, resort before the institutions of education or law enforcement step in, with those heavy-booted consequences. Often the mother's plea is that surely there must be something physically wrong with her child: Isn't there a diagnosis we can apply that will let us answer the dilemma or a pill that will cheer him up, make her concentrate, allow him to be happy to be at home, make her do what she's told?

You did what you knew. When you knew better, you did better.

—Maya Angelou

The themes that recur have to do with the burden that women feel obliged to carry. These themes relate to marriage failure and dissolution, an event from which few families are immune. They relate to guilt about raising the right kind of accomplished kids; they relate to feeling alone, unsupported, and pressured; they relate to finding themselves, like Charlotte, the spider in E.B. White's story *Charlotte's Web*, repairing, refashioning, and refreshing the web of relationships that bind the family together.

THE FALLOUT FROM MARRIAGE BREAKDOWN

At least 50 percent of the students in Canadian high schools are from what we used to call broken homes and which are now, in a salute to political correctness, never mind sheer numbers, called "blended" or, more recently, "extreme" families—a name that only masks the trauma of a failed marriage and its often painful aftermath. The family lines of these young people are cross-hatched with parents, live-in and live-out replacements, step-parents, and a flock of figures from a previous age who are called Grandma or Zaidy.

However, in our rush to blend one set of children with mother's new man or, more fractious still, with that man and his children, let us not forget the break that created these new relationships in the first place. The nature of a marriage that has gone bad or withered nearly always lies in the dysfunction of the couple, not the children. Back when I was first married, the rule was that you stuck it out for the sake of the children. Currently, couples believe they have far more leeway to dissolve the relationship and start anew, not just for themselves but also for the sake of the children. The trouble is, children are much slower to move through their issues of hurt, resentment, and mistrust of all things adult.

Supermom: A Predictable Response

Even if there is tacit agreement that the fire has gone out of their relationships, many of these patients soldier on, becoming supermoms in the process of becoming nonmates. So, not only are they devastated to find themselves replaced by the invariably younger, seemingly smarter, or more worldly version of the person they thought they were, they also are tired and often a little overweight. They do not host smart dinner parties, just Sunday barbecues with the family or grandparents. They do not see themselves as unattractive, just too busy to spend time or money on makeovers. Besides, for whom are they making themselves over? Life's routines are running their show, not the titillation of a weekend escape. They arrive in my office bitter, distressed, furious.

These feelings can often translate into mothering with a vengeance, and sometimes mothering with a vendetta, all hung on a prop of self-righteousness that inevitably crumbles into tears of frustration and hurt. So while the children feel mom's growing presence and her need to "do it all" (in order to protect them from their pain and fear), they rarely see her disintegration. That process is reserved for the late-night bottle of wine with a long-time girlfriend, or for the ear of the family doctor.

It takes time, patience, and some good counseling for women to be ready to try the relationship game again (more about this in the next chapter.) When they do, they are often wiser for their years, more honest in their expectations, and funnier about their own foibles. And since life really is about relationships, they connect with other equally bruised or battered partners to begin the serious work of building a new relationship.

But meanwhile, the kids are chanting the mantra, "Don't worry, mom. We'll be okay on our own." But will they be? Rarely. Will they act up? Almost certainly. It is just a question of how and when, and in which of thousands of documented ways. The less often asked question is: Will mom act up?

The supermom phenomenon can reemerge to inflict itself on her new mates' children in a most peculiar way. Enormously proud of the success and adjustment of her own children, she will—often against her better judgment—take even greater pride in comparing them with the problem-plagued children of her new man. Consequently, I frequently find myself listening to descriptions of the incredible manipulations that her mate's children are capable of exhibiting, behaviors seemingly evident only to her: "He's such a smart guy. I can't believe he's so blind to how they push his buttons and get him to do exactly what they want." Odds are, he isn't blind to his kids' manipulation of him. It's just that he's still protecting them from being hurt yet again.

The flip side occurs when the woman's kids are cutting up and the new man's are doing well—usually because his kids are often not living in the household, where the daily antics of sullen and inconsiderate behaviors are exposed. Moving a well-intentioned man into a teenage household is the signal for the adolescent to begin a particularly heated territorial battle. Often the children's fury at their father's disappearance from the home does not surface until another man walks in the door. At that point, adolescent raging hormones mix with a flood of child-like loyalty to defend the departed father. (Since it is almost never the mother who departs, mothers, it sometimes seems, do not require nearly the same loyalty quotient as fathers.)

Territorial battles surface in statements such as, "I don't have to listen to him. He can fuck off!" It is amazing to realize how the word "fuck" transits the rite of passage into adolescence, becoming the only meaningful word in a teenager's vocabulary. Certainly, in some conversations, it seems to frame every other word.

I have observed dozens of sons who stepped into what they perceived to be a breach in the family power structure to become the dominant male, albeit an angry one. Let me give an example. Some time after my newly minted husband-to-be moved in with me and my children, and before the wedding, battle lines were drawing up in our household between teens and adults. In desperation, and too aware that the impending marriage was an enormous factor, I called the wonderful Anglican priest and long-time family and addiction counsellor Brian Murray, who had conducted our mandatory prenuptial seminar. As we met in his office, we went into mode. My younger daughter and I wept, my older daughter ran interference, my son glowered, my man boxed. After 20 minutes, Brian got up and made me stand facing the children, putting Bob behind me. "Is this how you want to relate with your mother and Bob?" he asked. The children cheered. "Yes, he's not our dad and she needs to be our mom," they hooted. The session was pretty much over after that. Brian's parting words were, "What you owe each other is civility. After all, you are almost ready to leave home. You don't have to even like each other. Just be polite. You are still your mother's children."

While the advice is good it is not necessarily that easy to follow. These circumstances are complex and emotional. For us, the story still unfolds, but since my kids are now older, the pressures have declined. Remember, at some point after "letting them go," the kids do leave home!

Trusting Your Instincts

For most middle-aged moms, *not* trying to fix your child's problem is one of the hardest things you can do. Chances are, the need to "save" your child

> *In Canada, up to 5 percent of children have attention deficit disorder, while 10 percent have some learning difficulty.*
>
> —H. Steiner, Treating Adolescents

began for you (as it did for me, a mother of three) 15 or 20 years ago, when women started trying to shoulder it all: the career, the house, the kids, and, in our remaining time, the community volunteering, the just cause, the parent-teacher association. Since it was we mothers who shouldered a large portion of the responsibility for all that ailed our kids, it followed that we would bear a commensurate dose of guilt if the outcome of our efforts was not an unqualified success.

That guilt may have begun in preschool, when Johnnie didn't socialize well with his peers, or Tyrone didn't want to share his toys, and continued in elementary school, when Sally wasn't reading at her grade level and seemed inattentive and distracted. In an attempt to alleviate their guilt, mothers often want their children tested. Ironically, testing is rarely initiated by school officials. Usually it is I, as the family doctor, who gets questioned: Does Sally have a learning disability? Should she see a therapist? How do I make this go away? What do I do to fix this? Once the obvious indications for such testing have been eliminated, mothers find it hard to hear the word "nothing" in response.

As time passes, no one is more finely tuned, able to invoke the tiny volts of mother-guilt, than these same kids who have listened to the expressions of concern and self-doubt through the years. They know how to turn, with one word, even the most stalwart of mothers into a puddle of tears or raise a specter of self-doubt about the whole fabric of competent mothering, sending us all scurrying to the self-help section of the bookstore. The shelves are chock-full with answers to specific queries, like how to talk to the kids, how to get them to listen, perhaps even how to get them to wash—all part of the amazing process of what one of my patients calls "letting them go."

"AND SUCH A MOUTH ..."

One of my young patients was assessed at the Teen Crisis Unit at the Hospital for Sick Children in Toronto. Her mother was told that there was nothing wrong with her daughter, but the kid had the foulest mouth the staff had ever heard. In the process of this young woman's eruption, both home and school were abandoned. Phase one saw placement of this teenager in a group home and a residential facility, as well as two hospitalizations for concurrent illnesses. Phase two consisted of drug charges, incarceration, and giving birth to a baby boy as a single mother. And all by the time she was 16.

> *30 percent of teenagers in Canada admit to alcohol use; 5 percent admit to marijuana use; and 1 to 2 percent admit to using other illicit drugs on a weekly basis.*
>
> —*H. Steiner,* Treating Adolescents

Now in phase three, this young mother, single but not unsupported, is going to school again, is doing outreach work with street kids, living at home, and knows that her mother is her friend. Her mother, beside herself with guilt and fear during nearly a year of unrelenting domestic upheaval, still draws a blank about the factors that propelled such behavior in her girl. Her daughter has somehow managed to turn things around for herself, and her mother has held steadfast.

Another mom and dad threw themselves into a parent support group when their daughter decided to challenge all the rules of the household, as in, "No, I won't clean up. No, I won't accept your curfew. Yes, I will take drugs." While this couple were secure in their solidarity as parents, they needed the group to both spell out the consequences of this unruliness to their daughter ("If you don't want to live by the rules of the house, you will have to leave the house") and help them stick to their guns until things shifted. They knew in the end things would work out; they just needed a little extra steel in their resolution. Most parents do not go this route. And without such backing or counseling of some kind, they are carried along the chaotic path their child has set the family on, caught up in their guilt over everything they have done wrong.

If there is a single mom's version of this story, it emerges as that thinly veiled rage wafting from the children whenever the subject of her failed marriage comes up. The never-ending financial struggle, often after years of no struggle at all; the sense of abandonment; the failure to be good enough or to have pleased enough in order to hold the marriage together—all these issues that mom went through when the marriage first broke up now get to be played out again and again.

When mothers ask me for help with their acting-out teens, they are often already far along on the crisis curve. If Kate is skipping school, crisis management is the daily routine at home, especially when the school system has neither resources nor solutions for keeping Kate in class. I find myself listening hard. What has worked before? What resources have been useful? What books have they used? Which counsellors have they seen that they would recommend? What are the options? Their answers help build the resources for me to pass on to the next fretting mother I find in my office.

And always, after the tears, it comes back to trusting your own instincts. Trust your understanding of the natures of the children you've raised. That alone may be enough to hold you steady in your confidence that there will be an end to today's chaos, and that your children will remind you once again that they are what they are—a gift.

WHEN YOU'RE NOT HOME: DRUGS AND ALCOHOL

I've found that mothers are more accommodating about the sex issue than they are about the drugs. I had my eyes rudely opened this past year by the sons and daughters of my midlife patients. Many of these kids come in to my office and own up to their frequent use of drugs as blandly as they do to tooth brushing. I am not talking about 18 and 19 year olds, but 13 and 14 year olds. And I am not talking about experimenting with drugs on prom night or the weekend, but using them every day.

What I've learned is that the time of day can and does play a critical role in these behaviors and many other teenage traumas, from eating disorders and unsafe sex to using drugs and drinking. Just when you feel relief that your kids are not running amuck in the middle of the night, you realize there is another time zone to be concerned about. It is that "dead" zone between 4 and 6 o'clock when school's out and so are you. Most parents think of this time of day as safe. Not so.

For a lot of surprisingly young teens, the end of the school day is the signal to smoke up. Not cigarettes (they're bad for you and "way uncool") but marijuana, which is as readily available in schools as were the Pall Malls of my youth. When a young patient tells me braggingly that he, or frequently she, smokes weed, I sense something cocksure in this confession to the family doctor, for he or she is secure in knowing the information will not go beyond the office door. Confessing to smoking grass after school is cool. And the usual teenage conspiracy of silence about their behavior doesn't prevent my young patients from talking about "weed heads"—those kids who have a joint after school and who come down from their high in time to sit at the table with mom and dad and the sibs. A drop of Murine for the eyes and—dinner's served! Better still, by the time everyone's at the table or in front of the TV, these kids are having no problems at all, and their parents are grateful for the docility.

All teenagers think they are bulletproof when it comes to drugs. But with marijuana, that sense of omnipotence is even greater. Grass is the one drug that is deemed harmless and nonaddictive—an incorrect perception that can have nasty consequences, especially when you realize that today's marijuana is many times more potent than that of the 1960s and '70s. The apathy that

> *Accidents, of which those involving motor vehicles predominate, are the number one cause of teenager death. Alcohol plays a role in up to 66 percent of fatal MVAs in which teens are involved; other drugs account for 20 percent.*
>
> —*H. Steiner,* Treating Adolescents

occurs from smoking this super-grass results in both sliding grades at school and declining class attendance, and trying to stop smoking grass results in escalating anxiety.

The more familiar mischief involves alcohol. A 20-year-old patient of mine confessed that when she and her girlfriend were in grades seven and eight, they nipped into their parents' liquor supplies most weekends and many school nights to get drunk. They were even able to persuade a cab driver to purchase a bottle of whiskey for them by giving him a big tip. My surprise is a function of my denial. I know both these girls and the image I have of them. They are two of the most responsible young people on the face of the earth.

Sometimes, parents clue in to their kids' behavior because their kids are bad at physics, like the mother who kept her vodka in the freezer and presented a solidly frozen bottle to her astonished daughter, damning evidence that the teenager didn't know alcohol doesn't freeze—and that the daughter had been nipping from the bottle and replacing it with water.

But many parents do not clue in. This is because it is difficult to do so. While they may worry about their child's excessive fatigue, the disinterest in school, and the apathy, they can never pinpoint the cause. And after all, these characteristics are practically a definition of what constitutes a teenager. In fact, the last time a parent came into my office with a teenager who was complaining about excessive tiredness, we explored many things about the daughter's physical activity, her sleep, school, dance performance, and so on. All were seemingly dead ends as a root cause. I chose not to inquire about drugs or alcohol, though if I'd been alone with this young girl, I would have. Nor did I ask the mother to leave in order to make inquiries. After all, when the visit is over, the daughter still has to walk out of the office with her mother. It is a question of timing. Where drugs are concerned, it is usually only a matter of time before the evidence emerges. So it is essential to preserve a place where the teenager is not terrified to confess to drug use.

WHEN BEING THIN IS "COOL"

I recalled the need for this preservation of a safe place a little later when a 15 year old came in to see me on her own. Her friends had serious concerns about her eating patterns and told her that she was anorexic. Initially, she came seeking confirmation that her friends were overreacting. She and I have talked about her weight and her notions of body image in the past. But it was her current meal patterns that supplied me with the clue as to how the "dead" zone

> *13 percent of girls versus 6 percent of boys show disordered eating. Only 50 percent of anorexics and 15 percent of bulimics ever seek care.*

between 4 and 6 o'clock was figuring in the problem and, as a result, completely evading her parents' attention.

Like many teens, she is the first person home, arriving around 4:30. This is when she prepares and eats her own meal, something like half a Kraft Dinner, all by herself. So naturally, by the time her family is home and supper is on the table, she can claim she is full: she's had a huge Kraft Dinner and can't stuff another thing down. Mornings, it is off to early practice or to do extra work—those things that make parents comfortably assured that she is working hard, maybe even too hard since she is so tired. She eats nothing at breakfast and little at lunch. And half a Kraft Dinner just isn't enough to grow on.

But her friends blew the whistle on her. To keep them off her back, she came to her doctor, only to discover that I too was painting the picture of a very slippery slope. Her parents do not know of their daughter's eating disorder, and likely will not. They would be as shocked to learn their daughter has been living under their roof with an eating disorder as they would be if she confessed to dropping acid in her bedroom.

A teen hell-bent on tripping out, or descending into voluntary starvation, or hanging out all night in defiance of curfew, presents a frightening prospect for parents. What you as a parent need to know is that resources are available at every stage for practically every problem. It's easier to ask your teens if anything is wrong when the motive is curiosity and concern, rather than desperation, and when the field of action is instruction rather than incarceration.

So how can you explain your teen's irrational behavior? His or her whipsaw mood swings? The suddenly plummeting grades? Ogden Nash once wrote: "Oh what a tangled web do parents weave / When they think their children are naïve." Children are anything but naïve, however. Rather, they are masters at playing on the naïveté of their parents. There may be all kinds of benign reasons for changes in your teen's behavior. But I am constantly amazed at the number of parents who, though they suspect their kids are drinking or doing drugs, or have an eating

> *Suspicious signs of an eating disorder include a 10 percent or greater loss of ideal body weight, obsession with food and exercise, and recurrent dieting.*

disorder, refuse to talk about it—who don't even ask straightforward questions such as "Are you taking drugs?" They may get the truth in response. They may not.

"Don't ask, don't tell," may be the unspoken rule in many homes, but it is one that I believe should be broken. Especially at dinner, when your son or daughter is worryingly quiet—and not hungry.

LIFE IS A BASEBALL GAME— COVER ALL THE BASES?

Going it alone? Jenny, now in her early 50s, has been nursing her extremely sick husband for more than a year while holding down a job and raising two boys aged 19 and 15. She tells her story from the time she made the decision to adopt.

My natural son, Jason, was about 7 years old when I decided to adopt, and he was very much a part of the decision—wanting a brother or sister, he didn't much care which. I was single at the time, didn't see myself in any likely relationship, was too old for artificial insemination, and couldn't see becoming pregnant by stealth. Anyway, there were lots of kids who needed adoption. I took the course that the Children's Aid offers to families that are interested in older children adoption because they know these kids have problems.

It took a year and a half, and I reviewed the registry that is published twice a year from all the agencies. Paul's name had been on the master list in the fall and again in the spring, and I said clearly that I wanted to pursue adopting him. His mother was a junkie, and he had been taken from her when he was two. He was placed with an older couple; the woman had raised six children of her own, and they had left home by that time. It was her way of being a good Catholic and it was what she knew.

Paul was five and a half when he came to me, and he couldn't speak—at least nothing intelligible. Quickly, I discovered that he couldn't speak not because of any pathological reason but because no one had ever conversed with him. Nor had he had any kind of group interaction. So we got him into school pronto, even though it had been my intention to keep him home with me for the fall term. Over time, the severity of his learning disability became clear: his short-term memory, his inability to label or monitor his emotions, his fear of illness and loss—all of it lead to his acting out. Sure these older kids "put you to the wall" to see what it will take for you to throw them away like everybody else has done, but did I have any idea of how much or how long? I'll say not.

Going backward has never been an option for us. I knew we would never turn Paul back, so when people started suggesting that to Jason and me, it incensed us both. The first time this was suggested was when Paul (then seven) was incarcerated for a three-day observation period at Toronto's Hospital for Sick Children psychiatric. He had freaked out when I took him to the Children's Aid building to have testing arranged. I think he thought I was taking him back to the adoption agency and he had a major regression—tearing my clothes, throwing furniture in the waiting room—so they put him in the hospital. During conferences with the hospital staff and the school psychologist, my social worker said, "You can stop the process." She meant give him back. Jason was the one who shouted, "No one's taking my brother away," and I calmed him down quickly, before they all thought the problem here is the mother. I'm always afraid people are going to wonder about my motivation.

I've thought long and hard about Jason and his troubles now—some of them center around just being a teen, wanting to have a good time, and hanging out with the wrong crowd. However, I think some of his troubles have to do with how close we were before Paul came. I had been a single mom since he was four. In lots of ways, by marrying my husband I married my father, so to speak, who also had left my mother when we were kids. Both men were cut from the same cloth: charming, great raconteurs, a wonderful sense of humor, absolute womanizers, lousy husbands, terrible fathers, and financially irresponsible. I bent over backward to make it okay for Jason's dad to visit at every holiday. I never complained about missed support payments, I covered broken promises—there were plenty of those—all of which made Jason and I incredibly close, and made me determined to never break a promise to a kid. But as Paul acted out more, and the scenes became worse and took up more time, Jason became less and less sympathetic with his brother—the squeaky wheel getting all the attention. Jason became, and still is, an angry young man—angry at me, at his Dad, and at my new man.

That "new man" relationship really set things in motion, probably because Jason was 13 when it came to light, and of course the new man wasn't new—he is someone the boys have known all their lives. I didn't set out to have an affair, it just happened. Though my man has since told me that he had always been attracted to me, but never had acted on it. Anyway, this time he did and I did, and since there was some adultery going on, we didn't disclose until it broke wide open that Christmas Day when Jason was 13. Also, I think there are some real issues around his mother "doing it" ... most teens don't have to accommodate their parents' sexuality as they struggle with their own. You know your parents don't "do it" or if they do, "it's disgusting." But it's not an in-your face event. Along with that, he was jealous. "You always said you would tell me if you got a boyfriend," he accused. So the betrayal was big for him, as it was apparently for his dad, who also seems to have never quite relinquished his sense of territory. It was his father's display of rage that Christmas morning that gave both Jason and Paul a demonstration of how to tear a house apart and be verbally abusive.

My family has always been there as a strong support. My sister, and also my 82-year-old aunt—my surrogate mother after mine died of pancreatic cancer. The lesson has always been perseverance—you can't give up, you come from strong stock—always told by way of her own "horror" stories. She would take Paul, and I'd be afraid for her, but he was always perfectly behaved with her. She would take him to tea or the movies and drive around town showing him where she had grown up and gone to school. This is a kid who cuts himself, is physically very strong and has been violent, and who can throw himself down in the street and make out you've hit him—a real Mr. Hyde—but not with her.

My mother was a strong woman, worked hard all her life, finished high school at 15, and took a typist course before she got into university, where she studied child psychology. She was a nursery school teacher for a while. She and my father had a trial separation, though I didn't know it at the time. She went to London and worked for the Chinese news agency, living with two McCarthy-era refugee single mothers. I stayed in Toronto with my maternal grandmother, who ran a rooming house in the heart of Toronto. She didn't serve food, so it wasn't technically a boarding house, but we had the most amazing people living in our house. Ted Allan and Sid Gordon wrote the first book on Henry Norman Bethune, *The Sword, The Scalpel,* living in our house. Timothy Findley lived in our basement when he was a young man. Any number of actors—and gamblers—came through.

My grandmother was born in Jamaica in 1886, one of six bastard children produced from her father's liaisons with six different women. He had come out from England as an administrator, leaving behind his British family. None of these children, though, lacked for education, and in spite of being raised as Jews, they were sent to a convent school. And then my grandmother, who was very white, married "beneath her" to a very black man who was a champion cricketer and they had to get out.

My Scottish grandmother was equally strong in opinion and bias, and my mother, whom she considered colored, was never admitted into her home. Nor was my mother ever spoken to, though on my grandmother's deathbed apparently there was a picture of my mother, my sister, and me. My grandmother also moved her family back and forth across the Atlantic, I don't know how many times, never quite settling down, and she worked hard all her life to compensate for her sweet husband's alcohol problem. These family ties were always strong, since those relatives moved through my maternal grandmother's house so often. We just helped out family as they needed. So many single women raising kids in that household; but there was never any thought that we wouldn't go to university or have a career. Getting married and having kids was okay, but you had to rely on yourself. You've got to have that path for yourself, make sure you're stable. You can have the family support, but in the end you live alone, die alone, and you have to deal with it. So, while it wasn't easy dealing with all my problems, it wasn't anything that I didn't expect.

For sure I have badgered the institutions about Paul. Often they don't have the services they claim to have or the kid is the wrong age or they don't have the money. When he's been out of control—smashing up the house or hyperventilating—I've had him brought to the hospital, about three times, in police cars shackled and in ambulances strapped to the stretcher. It was during one of those times that he first heard a youth worker talking about "adoption breakdown"—something I never wanted to discuss because it wasn't an option. He asked me about it on our way to Children's Aid for one of our sessions. I was lucky with Children's Aid. The staff there watched him, were supportive, did an assessment. But he was an angel with them. In fact, that was when they thought that maybe I was the one who exaggerated or at least was the catalyst that sparked him.

Earlscourt Child and Family Centre was a God-saving grace for us. He was in residential placement there in grade six. They were always understanding and very knowledgeable. They had suggestions on how to try different approaches with adolescents; they never, ever made you feel that you had done anything wrong as a parent. They were really wonderful, and he flourished there. That was the other thing about Earlscourt. You actually find out you are not alone and that there are other parents whose stories are more horrendous than your own.

The really horrible time in my life was two years ago, when I fell in the door at your office to get the sick leave for work. My man had had emergency gall bladder surgery and then they found that cancer had gone through the wall of the gall bladder and were worried that it may have spread to his liver and pancreas. Jason had pedaled up to the hospital to get his allowance, and after that he wasn't home for six months because he was arrested for driving a stolen car and getting in an accident. He was still a minor at the time and, as it turns out, he took the rap for a friend who wasn't a minor, but as the police told me, they knew my boy very well indeed by that time. Anyway, Paul freaked out and threatened me with a knife because I wasn't going to bail his brother out of the youth holding center. One of the things that Paul has trouble dealing with is illness and separation. He and his new dad had bonded quite well, and the surgery and the cancer really frightened him. And then, with Jason arrested and me refusing to bail him out—because I thought he had to be responsible for his actions, plus I needed some assurances from him that he just wasn't giving me, so I let him stay a while, a couple of months all together—Paul just freaked. I think that was the time my aged auntie took him to her place for the weekend and he settled down.

At the detention center, we met with the social worker. Actually, I called for a meeting and asked them to put some schoolwork in place and counseling, and I asked Jason's dad to come. In truth, that's when I finished for good with his dad. He came to that meeting, didn't like what he was hearing from Jason, lost his temper, and stormed out. And after that I asked him for support payments for Jason. Do you know that because I hadn't got him to sign an agreement and Jason is now 19, he doesn't have to pay anything? So the kid is out some $40,000 in support payments, I figure.

They moved Jason pretty quickly to an open-concept jail downtown, sort of a group home, but it's a jail nonetheless. They have to earn the right to walk to the store for cigarettes. That's where he stayed for the most of the two months, and so now he has a record, and he was on probation for a year. He's working in construction now and will start back at school later this fall, and he looks great.

What do I think matters now? That Paul can label, and deal with, his emotions. He said to me recently that I should stop yelling at him because it makes him angry. That's amazing for him. And he can self-nuture—it's all around food. Always has been. He would pick up cookbooks at garage sales and ask me to cook dishes for him. We were doing homework today, and I'm so pleased with how he's handling it. It has never been about stupidity because he's not. It's been about him.

I realize that I've been 23 years on my job and that I can take early retirement in 2 years. What would I do? Work has always been supportive. I remember being in your office one day when someone needed to have a prescription for tranquilizers renewed and me asking, How come you don't give me any of those? Your reply was that I didn't need them.

It's not all bad news. In fact, it rarely is by the time the teen decade is done. Sure, many mothers are despairing right now over their teenagers and their misbehavior brought on by drugs, alcohol, or raging hormones. But what I said at the beginning of this chapter is just as true now—that all parenting is an exercise in hope. My experience is that even those teens who cause their parents enormous worry and grief somehow manage to traverse the precipices and reach the safe haven of their 20s fairly sane and happy, and, more importantly, capable of working to be happier. This is true for even those in the most discouraging situations.

The son of one of my patients, in an explosion to teenage rage, physically assaulted her. Yet now, six or seven years later, they have both come through this trial by fire, and her son is able to return home and reestablish a good relationship with his mother that permits her to support him returning to school—to make up for time and happiness lost.

8

STARTING OVER

Human beings have an inalienable right to reinvent themselves; when that right is pre-empted it is called brain washing.

GERMAINE GREER

Starting over in midlife is about finding the openings between the lines that seem to define our lives, the white space upon which one can imprint long-cherished dreams, restore one's soul, or reach for the stars. Starting over is about coloring outside the lines; doing new things or doing the same things differently.

There are no statistics for this phenomenon, no way to gather all the relevant information and evaluate how and why women, more often in midlife than at any other time, make certain choices that result in reinventing themselves.

What we do know is that in North America, a woman's life expectancy is now 30 years longer than it was in 1900. That's a generation longer. Consequently, in midlife, we can be looking forward to as many years ahead of us as we've already left behind. This extension of life has crept up on us, has opened new pathways and presented a fresh set of challenges and questions that may take some time to figure out. Can we have it all? Do we really want it all? What *is* all?

These are all weighty questions to which we are, and probably will be for some time, searching for answers. In the meantime, we are pushing the boundaries of life as our mothers knew it and are faced with a feast of variables which in their day would have been both unthinkable and impracticable, such as having a second child at 40-plus at the same time as grandmotherhood through the first child. Then there are relationship combinations that can make heads spin with confusion, from "my nest is empty but my new partner's is full" to two or three sets of step-children with whom various degrees of connectivity are maintained. And let us not forget career paths, keeping healthy, looking good (which usually means looking younger), caring for parents, and on and on. Little wonder that at some point we cry, "Enough!"

At that point, as one of my patients puts it, we start to repack our transparent suitcase—transparent because we and others can see the contents, which are constantly being rearranged and reviewed. In other words, there's a strong instinct for self-preservation that makes us review what we do and how we do it; and because we are no longer 25, there is a sense of perspective and, hopefully, a wisdom that governs that review. The subsequent changes we make can have enormous impact on our mental and physical health and on our souls.

THE SECOND — OR THIRD — TIME AROUND

Midlife love and marriage look and are different. Some women will start over by trying again, others by leaving behind a damaging relationship that has been held together for "the sake of the children."

Recently, I found a man whom I had once adored and lost. When we discovered each other again, I had already lived alone for many years. During that time, there had been the odd interlude and dinner "date"—a silly word for my age group—which usually ended before dessert was served. I had not been looking for a husband but certainly was open to the idea of a companion. However, as aging, eligible women in Canada outnumber ageless, eligible men almost two to one, I had no expectations of finding anyone. Frankly, even the notion of having to deal with the awkwardness of first intimacies didn't thrill me.

Then, suddenly, my soul mate of long ago reappeared, and for many months we talked, traveled, and rekindled a love that had only faded, never died. When we talked about living together, I was petrified and plagued with doubts. I immediately went into self-help (or self-flap) mode. The questions and the late-night conversations with friends were endless. After such a long time alone, I was set in my ways and free of having to make the compromises necessary to create good partnerships. In my disastrous 17-year marriage, I had felt compromised out of existence. Would I now be able to cope with another human being in my life?

> *Between the ages of twenty and forty we are engaged in the process of discovering who we are, which involves learning the difference between accidental limitations which it is our duty to outgrow and the necessary limitations of our nature beyond which we cannot trespass with impunity.*
>
> *—W.H. Auden*

Was I repaired enough and wise enough to fully engage in a new relationship? Would our two families blend, as they say, successfully?

I was forced into looking, for the umpteenth time, at my 17 years of married life. I was married at 21 and divorced at 38. What had I learned? I was now 55; would I be forgoing the inner peace I had created for myself? My marriage had been haunted by a terrible sense of aloneness. We had never really stood side by side when dealing with life's adversities and challenges. In fact, I came out of the marriage feeling that I had hauled and hewn and fetched water all by myself with the added weight of another on my back—not pleasant, and doubtless much of my own doing. However, when again in tandem, would I repeat this performance? Finally, there were only two questions that mattered. Did we trust each other enough to open up and work things out? Did I have the courage to start over?

We've been together a few years now and it's wonderful to know that I have the right person with whom to share my life. Now, I look forward to the future with joy rather than fortitude.

My patient whose story is told above is not alone. Most women stumble and are filled with angst over their reasons for getting married a second time, or a third for that matter, and not all such marriages have an outcome as happy as my patient's. However, the most interesting aspects of the stories I hear and which I retell here is the decision to try again, to start over with another human being, and to take a major risk at a time when we could be sitting back and deciding to live our lives alone rather than risk what we view as the possibility of failure, again.

My mother was well beyond middle age when she eloped, once again spinning the marriage wheel. She behaved in every fiber of her body like those nubile brides stepping up to the altar, radiant and expectant.

"So why?" I asked her. She peppered me with reasons.

"Because I don't want to be alone. Because he is good company and appreciates good food and cares how it is cooked. Because he has a good heart and likes to laugh. Because when your father was alive, he always took care to see that I was protected and that we didn't want for anything. Because your father and I were always a team and we worked together, and

I miss that. And because it is unseemly at my age to be living with a man and not be married."

They undertook to have a marriage contract drawn up by a lawyer. Neither financial considerations nor paranoia were behind their decision to do this. Rather, they knew that it would hold at bay the "heat" they were receiving from their grown children, who were cautious about preserving the well-being of their respective elders and aware of their parents' potential frailty.

By now, intensely curious about the phenomenon, I took the opportunity to ask everyone—friends, patients, myself—"Why?"

One big reason was "for the kids": so their children know that one marriage breakdown doesn't mean the pledges offered in matrimony aren't worth the effort or the hope. Ironically, another reason was, "Because I don't care."

Pardon?

"I mean, I'm not defined by being married any more, so if I choose to do it, it's because I want to and not because it's expected or necessary."

Most people seem to remarry because, this time, they want to do it right. As one of my patients told me, "I've now had the chance to know him, and I know that we can make it work."

One of the virtues of middle age is that we know ourselves so much better now. Many experts will claim that this knowledge is canceled out by the complication of lurking children and their well-documented role in splintering second marriages as often as they held together first ones.

But my experience is that blended families tend to do better when their new set of parents is married. There is something about the formal "permanence" of marriage that helps offset ninja attacks on that very thing. Problems of how the kids behave tend to get diffused and diluted when they are up against the parental stance of being in it for the long haul.

But most of all, I think we remarry because we feel life is somehow more real now than it was when we were 22. Or: "Because I want to live in a relationship that lets me trust again that it won't fail and know that I can risk that it might." Or simply: "Because I adore him."

Not Leaving, At Least, Not Yet

"I know that at some point I'll leave him, but for now, this is the best for all of us," said one of my patients after her husband told her that he had probably never really loved her, since who really knows what love is, anyway? He was thinking of living apart. There was no younger woman on the side. No job or health crisis. Just a profound internal malaise. Of course, his wife had noticed the slow, sure pace of his withdrawal after 15 years of wedded companionship, if not exactly wedded bliss. So this detached summation wasn't exactly a surprise. What really hurt was his solution of how to deal with their two teenaged children: he would move into an apartment, as would his wife into a different apartment, leaving the two kids in the marital home, in order not to disrupt their stability any more than was necessary. Not surprisingly, his wife sought counseling.

She refuses to leave the house, as does he. Toronto's landlords are absent two new tenants. The couple's two boys are as busy and as loved as they ever were. And it will likely be many years, if ever, that they will look back and wonder at what point something was different between mom and dad.

And the counseling? It took participating in an eight-week assertiveness training course led by a psychologist, along with a few one-on-one sessions, to address my patient's issues of self-esteem. Out of all this, she decided to take up an activity that had been only a dream, a fantasy really, given her matronly appearance and lack of physical activity. She decided to take up competitive rowing

Rowing suited her needs admirably, since practices were on Lake Ontario at 5 o'clock in the morning. Rowing in a scull with seven other women forced her into bed early; let her look after her sons, who didn't require car rides until later afternoon; and at the same time, sent the signal to the men in her family that they could now fit themselves around her schedule, thank you very much.

Rowing on a frigid lake in the dark before dawn solidified her sense of self-worth and activated all the rest of her considerable resources. Her work has improved dramatically. She has a vigor and enthusiasm noticeable by everyone. And her boys are doing well in school.

> *Rowing on a frigid lake in the dark before dawn solidified her sense of self-worth and activated all the rest of her considerable resources.*

"I never thought I'd be in this kind of relationship," she told me. "It only happened to other wives. My mother told me to keep rowing and never apologize for loving my boys. And looking after them right now is what counts most."

Another woman had been living with her man for many years. She owned a large, rambling house, had a good career, and, in her contentment, was growing overweight. She invited a friend who needed help getting back on her feet to move into the house and fill in the space. But life played a cruel trick, as it so often does. Her man soon had her friend off her feet. When the betrayal was revealed, my patient could have fallen apart. She certainly could have thrown them out. But she had a long talk with her lover's mother, whom she had grown close to and who revealed that, 40 years before, *her* husband had done the same. When she threw him out, she had to endure the anger of both their families.

Times do change. But my patient took a lesson from her lover's mother. This is why she allowed her ex-lover and ex-friend to find a place to stay before they moved out of her house. And since he's the one with a chronic illness and only intermittent employment, she feels no guilt. As she says, "It's not my way."

Was my patient a victim? Hardly. She felt badly enough to lose 25 pounds and start looking great again. But she couldn't afford to let her anger drive her life. She has her house back to herself and her self-respect. When I saw her last, she was more self-possessed than ever. In fact, she was positively cheery.

REDISCOVERING MOTHERHOOD

It was a reunion of sorts. My colleagues and I came together after 30 years to anchor our old work colleague as she reunited with her child who so long ago she had birthed and placed for adoption. Not that it was common knowledge to any of us in those far-gone days. At that time, we were a part of the 1960s therapeutic milieu in psychiatry. We were hot; we were on the edge; we were different. Thirty years has passed. And now Chantal is back in town and with purpose.

We meet up with Chantal at the end of the weekend and are introduced to her daughter, who is an image of her mother. We meet the daughter's family: husband and young son. We hear from Chantal about her weekend, starting with a get together with the adoptive parents—a means to get to know Chantal before the meeting, to suss her out? To prepare their daughter? To ease both these women into how they will wear a new relationship?

The time goes well but is wearing. The daughter's youngster gets sick and requires all his mother's time. Chantal waits impatiently with the calmness wrought of 33 years of waiting to hear if the boy is well enough to let these women proceed to walk together and talk. To ask the questions that have hung in the air for so long.

They do and it is done. Photo albums are exchanged. The next encounter is too tenuous a reality to frame yet. Like plowed earth, the event must settle, the seeds of the re-creation gain a hold to grow. But in this moment, Chantal has us wrapped with the threads of her story. She had fled her home and the family that was her strength and her bane. She found that she couldn't tell her mother she had become pregnant in a short, fast fling with an Afghani man who was now out of the picture, and not (by choice) any source of potential support. She was not an irresponsible girl. She stood at the door of the abortionist's office, money in hand, and could not go in. A friend heard of Chantal's plight and told her to come to the city, away from the village's eyes, where she could find work until the baby came and was put up for adoption. And so she came, working in the hospital as a psychiatric nurse, contacting the adoption agency, getting ready to pass through this dark phase of her life.

In time she birthed a beautiful baby girl. Briefly she pondered how she might support this baby. Would her cousin buy her house? She phoned, only to hear that her cousin had already bought another place. She said nothing. The day she left the hospital, she tried to walk into the lake. She was pulled out by the same staunch friend, who lay on top of her until she stopped thrashing and let the grief overtake her. Even after so many years, the story's retelling had the power of wrenching heartache, of blind pain and anguished loss.

It was shortly afterward that the new psychiatric unit where Chantal worked began to be configured with the latest models of care. Staff initiated a multitasking approach, doing group work in-house and outreach work in the field; patient-staff councils were created; and shared decision making was enlisted. In short, a therapeutic milieu was created. Into this ferment she walked with grace and refinement, her English formal and tentative, her demeanor elegant and calm. She was our "mother" model. Patients helped her understand the idioms and the vernacular of the group sessions. She was attentive and polite and evoked the same response from even the most irascible or sickest patients. And for the families, she was a refuge and a comfort in the rat-a-tat-tat of the ward banter. Always a musical quality accompanied her spoken word and always there was the infinite patience and expectation of civil behavior.

Now, after 30 years, she recounts that she was never able to leave home or go away on a trip or come home after her work without having the expectation that something was about to happen. A phone call. Something. Always waiting.

Some years ago, Chantal wrote to the adoption agency to see if she could contact her child. The agency said that the choice to contact her rests with the child but that they would forward a letter from Chantal. No word, and for years Chantal lived believing her girl did not want anything to do with her. But last year, her daughter initiated her own search. Chantal's letter was on file in the records of the adoption agency. The adoptive family had lived abroad for a number of years, and Chantal's letter had never been forwarded.

To prepare for the encounter, Chantal welcomed young people into her home. "The more the merrier," she said. She needed to hear how young people talked and what they talked about. She was in the same stance she had been so many years ago—attentive, listening, understanding. The young people knew what was up, and their interest was piqued. They coached her and encouraged her and reassured her that she couldn't fail to win the heart of this long-lost child.

We talked long into the night as she relived all the stories, all the lost leads, the aftermath of waiting yet to come, of waiting to see and be seen, of waiting to connect, again.

The adoptive parents were one bridge, we were the other, each in its way holding these two women up for each other, cushioning the terrors, providing a haven for the memories.

Chantal is back home now, and feeling the deflation that must accompany so much effort, so much expectation, finally realized. But now when she goes home she knows what call she is expecting, and it will come.

Starting Over in Work and Career

According to Statistics Canada's 1996 census:

- In 1996, Canadian women comprised nearly half the workforce.

- 182,675 men (15 years or older) spent 10 or more unpaid hours per week caring for seniors, compared with 361,885 women (15 years or older).

- 698,160 men spent between 15 and 29 unpaid hours per week caring for children, compared with 836,100 women.

A significant number of working women are also the sole providers for their family. The millions of dollars in outstanding child support payments are a clear indication of both the financial and emotional burden these women bear.

In addition, much work remains if we are to achieve the goals of equal opportunity and equal pay set by the feminist movement in 1960s and '70s. Statistics Canada's *Women in Canada* (3rd edition, 1995) states that in 1993, at all levels of educational attainment, women's earnings were lower than those of men. Even female graduates employed full time, full year, earned only 75 percent of their male colleagues' salaries.

Nor have we begun to examine the true worth of woman's unpaid work, as indicated in the above figures: child care, elder care, shopping, housework, and so on. In the last 80 years or so, much has changed and little has changed. Like our mothers, who worked in factories, offices, and shops; looked after the home and family; and took typing and business-school courses in order to get ahead, to have financial independence, to support the dreams of their families, we do much the same thing today, with many of the same goals for our families.

> *In 1991, more than 80 percent of all single parent families were headed by women, a figure that has remained relatively constant since the 1960s.*

Today, we prepare our children for the likelihood of having some five different careers in their lifetime. However, this is not a concept with which we grew up, even though it seems we should have. We were told that we should have a career and that switching jobs too often was a sign of unreliability, rather than a desire to explore, climb, or advance. Consequently, many of our generation have been unprepared for the massive changes in business and the economy.

As a result, women come to my office in enormous distress because they are unprepared for finding themselves downsized, redundant, and outsourced—especially after 20 or 30 years of being on the job, day after day, year after year. They are unprepared and their distress has as much to do with being middle aged as with suddenly finding themselves back in the job market. How women cope with this challenge has been both one of the great fascinations in my practice and a solid testament to the resiliency and spirit of women. Resiliency is a word that researchers have used to describe an attribute required to overcome adversity. It has been used to account for unexpected outcomes in trauma, violence, and populations subjected to acts of genocide but is not usually applied to women who are considered well heeled, well trained, and resourceful.

There is no doubt that losing what has been a life-defining job at midlife is stressful. What has to be ascertained is the potential for this stressful situation to create distress and dysfunction, determined by far more than visiting one's physician. From the comfort of my office chair, I am constantly amazed by the ability of these women to turn a nerve-wracking circumstance into a liberating change.

As our mothers so rightly knew, job skills are portable and can be applied in any new job. In other words, you can do the same job anywhere. A typist is a typist is a keyboarder. A clerk is a clerk is a scanner. But a lot of middle-aged women are different as they re-enter the job market. They are tired of making the boss look good, of being the platform from which everything else springs—tending to the details, taking care of loose ends, and catching hell when things don't go well. In the new job arena, certain attributes are seen as negatives: they are too old to train, they are frumpy, they are rigid, they don't want to work 12-hour days to impress the boss (indeed, they no longer feel the need to impress the boss), they don't dress to a code. Other attributes are enormously useful and valued for what they represent in business. They come with references, they will do menial jobs, they will expect less in return than the all-stars, they are loyal (seemingly without reason or reserve). Above all, they will work at a good rate—for the company.

Some of my patients play along with that game, conserving their energy for other, more important, life tasks. After all, they may need those financial resources to look after their parents or one or their kids. So they will take the job in order to assure themselves that they have the ability to provide for their dependants. However, if at this time in their lives they have the freedom to choose, or have cobbled an opportunity, or are able to indulge (the sensual connotations of the word belie its virtue) in the realization of a dream, it is a very different and powerful life force to witness.

Climbing Mountains

For a thousand reasons it shouldn't have worked. It was improbable. It was untested. It was expensive. Three midlife women, each of them in a state of personal transition, came together with an idea. In a blaze of like-mindedness and shared values, and in a mere two months, they were marketing the Rock to Grow experience to corporations.

> *Inviting other women on an intense 48-hour journey usually requires having a reassuring answer to the question they will inevitably be asked: "How often have you done this?" Not for these women.*

One of these women is a former invest-ment banker for the Asian market, who for 16 years had been at her desk before 7 o'clock in the morning. Two years ago, she walked away from the pressure and the money and began to refashion her life and mission. That latter word is one she now uses frequently, as she is totally focused on helping other women change their lives in midstream for no reason other than it *is* midstream.

The second woman has always been a seeker. Trained in kinesiology, she has explored therapeutic touch, Brain Gyms for kids, running, bike touring, teaching yoga, vision questing, stretching all her boundaries in search of some universal truths and their practical applications.

The third woman is the "detail guy" of the trio, reinventing her entire life after a rare drug reaction left her permanently disabled. She has yet to deal with the 20 business suits in her closet.

What this trio possessed in enthusiasm for their idea more than made up for their lack of experience. Inviting other women on an intense 48-hour journey—one that was way beyond their comfort level—usually requires having a reassuring answer to the question they will inevitably be asked: "How often have you done this?" Not for these three women.

After an evening seminar with one of Canada's top female mountain climbers, off we went for a day of rock climbing on the cliffs, two hours north of Toronto. Getting to the top of the cliffs and back to the bottom safely was only half the exercise. We then had to apply what we'd learned

("Never get a manicure *before* you go rock climbing!") to the stern realities of the office.

But Rock to Grow wanted to pamper its clients as well as challenge them. So, back from the rocks, dirty and tired, we took respite at an inn that can only be described as your very wealthiest friend's weekend retreat, and nestled in the finest linens. On the second evening, there was a wine tasting, followed by a dinner, with one of Canada's most renowned chefs cooking up a feast—and putting the women to work as his sous-chefs. This is creativity and challenge of a very different kind, but is it more than just high-toned fun and games? I was skeptical beforehand. But I'm a convert now. Why? Because I believe that women who share extreme experiences (whether on the rocks or in the kitchen) use them and grow through them in ways that are mysterious.

In a previous encounter with Outward Bound, I had experienced the bonding that comes from embracing a physical challenge designed to stretch you beyond all expectation. Doing so in the company of others who are equally terrified, you find, at the very least, soul mates for life. When, after being out in the bush for five days in the dead of winter, we boarded the small plane home from Thunder Bay, we asked the flight attendants to fasten us to the wings and we would fly *them* home! As we get older, there are not many opportunities to feel that kind of exhilaration, and the occasions are memorable for a long time afterward.

The Rock to Grow adventure was different. It was more compressed, woman-centric, and, from the outset, focused on a clearly stated set of goals. Our efforts were consistently directed and marshaled to reach those goals, and while the leaders acknowledged that highly emotional states might surface from the experience, they encouraged us to accept them and move on. In other words, to get on with it!

But what did the women bring to the venture that ensured such success? I think it was an obvious readiness to change, something midlife women seem to thrive on. My experience is that women aren't likely to ante up for the challenge of doing something for which they have no experience or of which they are terrified unless they are prepared to have a different outcome in their behavior or self-esteem. Even then, most of the women in our group were unprepared to lean on other women in order to achieve that goal. These particular women pride themselves on being self-reliant, self-made, independent—sole proprietors of their success.

As we stood at the bottom of the rock face, two of the women in the group were clearly petrified of the daunting heights that rose ahead. Despite all our encouragement and shouts of "one more toehold and you've got it," what got them to the top of the cliff was their own gumption to go, as one participant put it, "one step beyond" their fear. What gave them this courage to push ahead was the chance to take a break or to take a boost, both options provided by the rope that held them. And, as for the strong anchor woman who was your "buddy" as you hoisted yourself upward on the rock face, there was an inordinate sense of responsibility, especially for the well-being of those who were most frightened or doubtful of their capacity and courage.

Lots of women these days climb cliffs, real or metaphoric. What made the Rock to Grow experience so meaningful was not what happened on the rock face but what occurred afterward. We did something much more daring and consequential. We talked to each other. After the cliffs, the wine tasting, and the dinner, we began to talk about our hopes and fears and, under the gentle prodding of our trio of leaders, we confessed the nature of the one thing we needed to do in our personal lives, the one "action item" we had to deal with in order to move forward and not stay mired in old patterns and resentments.

One woman talked about what was really keeping her from reconstructing her business. Another, who had dreams of writing, explored her option not to return to her national sales job. We all shared those fears and committed to an action plan. The result of which led me to have a panic attack on the drive back to Toronto, something I had not experienced in at least 10 years. It took me a few days to sort out, but eventually it became clear that the time was right to open old baggage and clear out some of my old fears.

All of us knew how to make these changes—we just needed other women to witness and to help keep our courage up after we'd all gone our separate ways. And that's what happened. Two weeks after the dinner and talk, there was a two-hour conference call during which everyone checked in on the progress of the others. We hadn't all done what we'd committed to. But enough of us did—a testament to the incredible catalysts women create just by allowing themselves to share an intensive experience.

One of the greatest of these forces for change is the connection that women can provide each other. It is true that there is now an industry that is best described as providing midlife women with certified personal coaches and midlife counsellors. These are service-driven organizations that have emerged to answer the needs of an increasing number of women who are forced, yearning, or stumbling to seek new directions. For the most part, these services are not free, but if we view the middle managers in a large firm as commodities, susceptible to outplacement, then the rationale is there to pay for such services. But do women need or require such a service in order to move on? My answer, based on experience, is an emphatic no. As I hear the stories unfold in my office, I am most impressed with the elusive quality of resilience that shines from most of my patients, along with their humor and an abiding faith in the rewards of hard work.

As women realize that their age is now their ally, not their shame, other sources of strength emerge. And, while it will take time and a few more millions of these women of a certain age before resources and policy move in a direction that favors them, it will happen, especially as women come together to share and work with their individual resourcefulness. That is networking on a large playing field. As Gloria Steinem once said, "One day, an army of gray-haired women may quietly take over the earth."

Getting Out in Your Prime

No one commands respect like one of my patients, a special-education teacher who is a mother of four. The term "factored out" has always struck me as a misnomer since many of my patients are not only not let go but actively seek to get out at the earliest possible date. Many a teacher who sits in my office can recite, to the day, the time left before she can take early retirement. The same can be said of many midlevel bureaucrats working in government offices. Where industry has permitted the famous factor 80 or 90 (if present age plus years of work equal 80 or 90, you can retire) to evolve—as a means of what? reward or removal?—it now has created a peculiar state amongst midlife women, and men as well. Most of the teachers I see are by now at their peak, and not only for teaching. They have experience, dedication, and smarts. The same applies to all those government workers.

So why are they rushing to the door? To no one's surprise, they will tell you it's because they're tired. Tired of the increasing expectations, the lack of power, the time constraints, the numbers, the shrinking resources, the doing more with less. They have all felt the burden of their work increase as their supportive infrastructure vanished. They have felt their idealism shrink as they have been devalued and equated to some variant of a production quotient. They have arrived at a time in life when they have most to give and nowhere to give it. Simply recognizing this new reality should mobilize another enormous talent pool.

> The term "factored out" has always struck me as a misnomer since many of my patients are not only not let go but actively seek to get out at the earliest possible date.

These people are not retirees in the traditional sense. Most, in fact, return to their usual occupations—teachers to teaching, managers to contractual stints—but in a more constrained and limited fashion. Some will apply their talents to other enterprises. All will show that not only are they not tired but, surprisingly, they have unbounded energy. They will demonstrate the regeneration of a cloaked enthusiasm that enlivens and creates sparkle.

One of my patients did high-level data entry for a provincial ministry for 15 years. As the branch where she worked shrunk through repeated downsizings and reorganizations, she took the severance package offered her because she couldn't bear going into work every day and reinventing her job. She used all of her lump-sum severance package to take one year of intensive computer-upgrading courses and counted on her husband's salary to carry them both in the interim. She had the usual anxieties: Was she too old? Was her English (not her first language) good enough? Was she marketable in a young person's job market? Was she smart enough (when a pass was 90 percent because of the standards of these high-tech web masters)?

After a year, she completed the course and began her job search. It wasn't easy. She wasn't what the market wanted in the hey-day of tech-wizards; she couldn't devote endless hours to dot-com start-up firms with grand expectations but no guaranteed salary. Her husband became sick and was forced to leave his work prematurely on a meager pension. Still, she struggled on, going to a community-based Internet job-placement resource. This strategy got her out of the house every day and kept the routine going. As the resources dwindled, she took a contract job at her old ministry and, as she tells it, went to work every day and looked busy.

One day, she noticed a posting for a senior-level job in her department. She told her boss that she would like to apply. Out of 300 candidates, she was one of 6 after the first round. At the end of the second round, she was 300 points ahead of her nearest rival. She took the job and still "goes to work and looks busy." This is a woman who needs to be able to retire to do good work.

Downsized but Not Down-pressed

I see women who are the big earners in two-income households suddenly thrown off the fast track and into the embrace of an outplacement counsellor. However big their severance package, it seems that it is never enough to forestall a downsizing of their family's lifestyle or a discreet dip into the RRSPs to pay for today rather than tomorrow.

> *Women are used to reinventing themselves every few years ... Changing is what most women have been doing all their lives.*

None of these women is ready to retire. They have decades of active living ahead of them, and very few have put enough money aside to see them even a few years into that journey.

So where do these women go? What do they do? Some become entrepreneurs, not because they've thought of themselves as particularly energetic, independent, or driven by a dream. Rather, they do so because they're so used to reinventing themselves every few years in large bureaucracies that they have little trouble doing so now. Besides, changing is what most women have been doing all their lives. The jobs and variety of paths that have been a part of one patient's story are in themselves a how-to manual on changing roles as we roll through life. Nor has change always involved big outlays of money or a return to school.

This woman began as a housecleaner and from there launched a cooking service for clients. She would ensure that there would be a home-cooked meal for the family two or three nights each week. However, in time she wanted something different, so her next job was with Outward Bound, where she was the cook for one of their many Home Places. From there, she returned to the city and signed on as a chef, a particularly rigorous and risky career move, all things considered. Given that restaurants were opening and closing in equal numbers, it was no great surprise to her that she was, eventually, laid off.

Rebounding from this setback, she used her tiny severance package to enroll in a web-design course. In this, as in all things she has cooked up, she has shown her talents and now has her dream job designing websites for small nonprofit organizations. On occasion, she still offers her services as a cook, or pitches in and works like a field hand. Her motto is that the whole is more important than its parts.

Another of my midlifers is also in the serious business of reinventing her life. She had emigrated to Korea on a personal two-year adventure to teach English as a second language. Packed up, uprooted, ready for a singular adventure into another culture, another way of being. I had heard from her daughter that she was returning some six months later, but it was not until she arrived in my office that I got the scoop on her decision to bail.

She did not leave because of the loneliness or the tendency for ex-pat partying in her small apartment building to go on until the small hours of the night. Nor was her decision based on cultural differences, as so often is the case when female English instructors are engaged by companies in the Pacific Rim countries with different, sometimes sexist, cultural practices. No, surprisingly, it was because she could not tolerate the money-grubbing attitude of her employer who, it turned out, gave not a wit for the actual instruction being delivered to the pay-for-English students. "Hard drinking, hard living, incredibly sexually preoccupied" was the way my patient critically described the director—a woman—running the service.

My patient recognized that the director was in serious conflict with her values about both education and content. Also, my patient was having difficulty in a culture that is often oblivious to the hard-won rights of women that we of the West now take for granted. Her male students could not even begin a discussion around AIDS or sexual transmitted diseases—the concept of responsibility at any level was totally foreign. Nor did they hesitate to openly discuss their mistresses in the same breath as their wives. So she came home, seemingly with little to show for her efforts and a lot lost in the process.

Does she feel defeated in realizing her dream? Not at all. This restart is serious business, and there is no time for regret or recrimination. She is now comfortably ensconced in the nanny cum granny-pad in her daughter's home. She is doing pick-up jobs as a census-taker and working evenings on a contract with the local hospital as an intake person. She does not provide primary care for her 22-month-old grandson, but she is a steady backup and much appreciated in those off-hours. And she is enjoying watching him grow. But is he her modus of starting over? Not by a long shot! She will retool, reestablish, and reinvent herself anew.

There are thousands of similar stories. Forced to leave careers that have turned to ashes in their mouths, women now have the peculiar freedom that straitened circumstances or society's indifference brings—to do what they've always really wanted to do. Often, this is something very small, focused, and even intimate, the very opposite of what they've been striving for or forced into during the last 30 years.

9

PARENTING YOUR PARENTS: CARING TO THE END

I look in the mirror and, shockingly, find the first lines of unwelcome similarity, the creases and folds of an unacknowledged heritage, and while I do not see a close resemblance—I see my mother's fear, and learn that it is never too late for compassion.

ANONYMOUS

However long we have carried or, in some cases, lugged our parental baggage, and regardless of our age when first we start to sense the profound shift in the relationships with our parents, the sooner we unpack that particular suitcase, the greater will be our wisdom in approaching the loss of the most influential relationship of our lives—for good or ill, love or hate. At least that's the theory, but somehow the timing is always off.

> *For the first time in Canadian history, most people have more parents living than children.*
>
> *—Statistics Canada, 1992*

When I first talked to my editor about this chapter, she was concerned that it might be prescriptive. I wouldn't presume! Millions of words have examined, evaluated, imagined, crafted, and analyzed from every perspective this most fundamental of relationships; many excellent books deal with the practicalities of legal and financial planning; assessing nursing homes and the myriad care options and decisions that seem to suddenly creep up and slap one in the face. There are even consultancies that specialize in creating a profile of your parents' needs and advising on what is available based on your and your parents' income.

But I can't ignore the fact that women spend almost double the amount of time that men do in caring for a senior. More than half these women will have both full-time jobs and children living at home. In 1998, 3.7 million people in Canada, or 12.3 percent of the population, were seniors, and since that number is to expected to increase to 22.6 percent by 2041, the ramifications for middle-aged women are enormous.

This chapter is about the child becoming "father of the man," about growing up or out, about listening and accepting the wishes of others—beloved or not. It is about letting go and being let go; it is about accepting responsibility.

HER DEATH, HER WAY

Sarah is a wonder, and I listen enraptured as she unfolds the story of her mother's decision to die—in her own way and her own time. She was not a well woman and had already suffered a small stroke and a heart attack before a further series of strokes put her in hospital—far too disabled for her liking. That's when she decided to die. The first inkling that Sarah got of this resolution was when her mother passed her some pills, telling her to hide them quickly before the nurses saw them. "Eh what," Sarah said. "What are these? What are you about?"

She was told to hush and not make a scene, but already she was shrill with indignation. "You can't do this! What are you thinking? I'm not going to stand for this. Don't you know you will die?" Their voices rose and soon all the long ward of frail, elderly women was enlisted by Sarah's mother in admonishing the disrespectful conduct of her unruly child.

"I just didn't get how she could make that decision. She was only in her 50s. But she had decided and so she stopped eating. It took her three weeks. Along the way, the hospital staff discussed options with us for force-feeding her—tubes and intravenous and all—but we just couldn't see doing it to her when she was so adamant. As she weakened, my sister and I tried to talk her into eating by getting her a favorite "pees-pudding" sandwich. She chewed and chewed and then spat it in our faces, railing at us not to try that again. Toward the end, the staff moved her to a private room—her behavior had so deteriorated that no one was safe from her caustic remarks. Eventually, she was left with only her "angel," her own mother, who seemed to come more and more to spend time with her as she lapsed into a coma. I didn't understand it then, but as I think about it now I realize that her life was more complicated than I knew. The determination to just do what she did, it's a wonder to me now."

Sarah's story highlights one of the biggest issues surrounding dying with dignity—the right to choose. We are not talking here about active euthanasia (from the Greek, meaning a good death), whereby there is deliberate intervention to end a person's life, such as administering a lethal dose of sedatives to someone with a terminal illness, but rather an inactive euthanasia, whereby treatment is withheld or life support is turned off, thereby allowing the person to die naturally.

Much of the present controversy about whether individuals have the right to choose the time and manner of their death has centered on incurable and degenerative diseases, rather than on old age. However, as demographics shift and people live longer, their chances of frailty and disease increase—often eroding their independence. So, while advances in medicine may prolong life, they do not necessarily improve or even maintain the quality of life. And, some would argue, that life is occasionally preserved against the wishes of the person involved. Many groups feel that present laws need reviewing, especially in the light of both medical technologies that can sustain life indefinitely and the evolution of palliative care.

In 1999, women accounted for 57 percent of all Canadians aged 65 and older; 60 percent of those aged 75 to 84; and 70 percent of those aged 85 and older.

Doubtless, the debate will rage for some years before a consensus is reached. In the meantime, a person in Canada can express his or her wishes in advance by giving directives or by designating someone to have power of attorney for health care should that individual be unable to express his or her wishes.

No matter how prepared we are for the inevitable, attending to the care of our parents is always distressing and difficult for midlife women. It turns us again into caregivers at the very time when, for many, those days were meant to be over, and stretches our schedules as well as our sanity to the breaking point.

I have seen patients drop everything, including their job and family, to rush home to care for a parent who is suddenly helpless and in need of urgent attention. This may involve closing apartments, clearing the family home and its years of accumulated memorabilia, arranging for care, or the dreaded word—institutionalization.

One of my patients, a single mother, put her fledgling business on hold and, with a hefty student loan outstanding, flew to her native country with her ailing mother in tow, reestablishing her in the ancestral home. She hired a contractor to enlarge the windows, put in air conditioning and toilet facilities, and arranged for round-the-clock nursing. Her mother was terminally ill and her death was imminent. When my patient returned to Canada after delivering her mother home to die, she had to renegotiate her rent and the reconnection of her phone line. And she knows that when the call comes, she will board a plane again and return for the burial, this time leaving her two boys at home in Canada. She knows too that she has already done "the right thing."

Another of my patients traveled to the United States to arrange her father's entry into a nursing home after a stroke left him too impaired to continue on his own. For her, this meant securing power of attorney, reinstating a long-lost social security number and green card, closing down the hardscrabble apartment that had sustained him for years on his own. All this for a man she had barely known in the 25 years of her adult life; a mean man who had left the family early on. She too is sure she's done the "right thing"—putting to rest some of her tangled and fractious relationship with her father. She will not return to the United States when she gets word of his death—it will not be necessary.

THE LIVING ARRANGEMENTS

Some of my patients would rather deal with their parents' death than with the hugely guilt-inducing exercise of putting them into a nursing home, which both parties view as a necessary evil, or worse, a living grave. Since most elders haven't lived, as elders, with their offspring in the first place, Canada lacks a community care model that sustains the frail, elderly living in the homes of their children, with professional caregivers relieving the adult children.

> *Some surveys suggest that baby boomers likely will spend more years caring for a parent than for their children.*

While our aging parents may defend their failing strength, vitality, and independence in front of their disbelieving children, what they really fear is dependency on the goodwill and care of strangers. For those midlife children, as well, it is hard to turn that care over to strangers because they are just that, strangers, and no one understands mom like her kids. So, sometimes, a retirement facility that takes parents from the state of "elderly independence" all the way to full and secure nursing care works to ease these transitions, and the guilt.

One of the consequences of Canadian women now living to an average age of 80 plus is the many levels of care that may be needed as these women's capacity declines. The physical deterioration is obvious. But the mental deterioration of a parent, and their regression into senility, is much more disturbing for adult sons and daughters to observe.

An estimated 22.4 million US households—nearly one in four—provide care to a relative or friend aged 50 or older or have done so during the previous 12 months.

—National Alliance for Caregiving and the American Association of Retired Persons

Yet, I've had patients take their aged parent out of a nursing home and assume the grinding process of 24-hour care themselves. When I questioned one of these dedicated caregivers about why she would want to spend money on supplementary oxygen for her mother when it was not necessary and would not delay or ease her mother's demise, she assured me that her mother did better on it and, anyway, it was her mother's money. That is, it was a choice made by and for the mother.

Moving Mother in with You

Approximately 15 percent of seniors aged 80 and older live with one or more of their children. According to 1993 statistics, this proportion was twice as high for women (19 percent) as for men (9 percent).[1] Making the decision to have a parent move in with you is always complicated. There is much to consider: Is there enough space for folks to get away from one another? How will access to common areas work? and so on. What happens when a midlife woman moves in with a parent? Which way round is it? The following story illustrates an unusual circumstance, one that is unlikely to become commonplace but which may become increasingly typical.

I was already at Mom's house at least twice a day unless I was out of town, which was not often. Between checking Mom on my way to work and taking in dinner at night, shopping, going to the drugstore, or taking her for doctors appointments, there isn't a lot of time that is my own. Plus, even though there is a nurse in attendance twice a day, the nurse is in and out, and if there is anything that concerns her, it is up to me to arrange a visit and have a discussion with her.

Mom and I talked about selling both our houses and moving into a new bungalow that would be disabled-friendly, but it would take all her resources from the sale of her house as well as mine to do this. So, renovating my home seemed a better alternative. Of course, the project grew day by day in terms of our wish list so that, in the end, the cost came to around $70,000. By selling her home and putting that against the reno-vation, Mom was left with a small cache of money, which was very important to her. To be fair, all of us three sisters agreed that this was the best arrange-ment and decided that if anything happened to mother before the deed was done, my expenses would be covered out of the house sale before any will came into effect. For my part that was essential, since I didn't have that kind of reserve cash to do the renovation without mother's money. My sister's felt it was both a good investment and a fair exchange for my being the responsible caregiver. It will be easier not to be running back and forth,

> *According to a 1993 national survey, approximately 30 percent of those 65 and older and 37 percent of those 80 and older reported receiving assistance from a daughter.*
>
> *—National Health and Welfare, Canada,* Ageing and Independence

trying to keep up both places—watering, planting, weeding, etcetera. Just the upkeep alone on the two houses was wearing me out.

My bathroom moves into the basement, but it is a wonderful big space. We decided on mirrored glass doors for the access into the water heater. And there is a large linen closet. The room is right at the bottom of the stairs and gets its light from both a win-dow and the stairwell to the kitchen. Mom's bathroom is off her bedsitting room and is wheelchair accessible for both toilet and shower, even though she doesn't require a wheelchair yet. It's lit via a wonderful skylight. As well, there is a big deck off Mom's room and in the newly configured kitchen-family room there will be a new stove, fridge, microwave oven, and, for the first time ever (for me), a dishwasher.

The neighbors could not have been nicer. Once the water and electricity were shut down (because of the renovations), they began to water the lawn, and so on. And they were generous about offering their electricity when the workmen required additional power. They are delighted about Mom moving onto the street. Since it's only three blocks from her old house, even those neighbors have assured her that they will be around to see her ensconced in her new digs.

While having Mom under my roof will ease certain burdens, it will undoubtedly create others. For instance, my long-term relationship with Sam will change. We each have our own homes, and there was nothing nicer for me, when arriving home late at night, than seeing his car in the drive. I knew he would just come by and make himself a coffee and settle in waiting for me to come home, watch the news, have a bite, stay the night or not. That won't happen now. He will never just walk in on Mom; I know that. I'm not sure what it will mean, but I do know it is going to change and it makes me mad.

Then there's my daughter, who looks at the new space and is already saying she should just move back home with her kids. I have taken care of one, and occasionally both, of my grandchildren every weekend for most of their lives. I drive to Belleville on Friday night, pick them up, and bring them to my house, and tuck them in their own room. On Saturday, either I take them out or we do crafts and projects in the house. When I go to church, I take them to Sunday school, and afterward I either take them back to their mother or she comes by to collect them, and sometimes has dinner with me. I tend to try to keep these activities away from Mom, as she finds the kids noisy, and her routine is pretty rigid—so she won't wait on her meals for people to gather.

Looking after these children, who are nine and seven, is my way of trying to help my daughter. The relationship between us hasn't always been an easy one and I, for one, have struggled with trying to make her happy and feeling badly when her life is disruptive. I love my daughter and those kids and will do just about anything to help them. I know I do too much sometimes, and I end up feeling resentful, angry, and guilty—worrying that whatever I do, it will never be enough. So, I'm not sure how that relationship will work out when Mom moves in. Mom has said she will just go to her room, but already I can see her impatience with the kids now that I'm staying in her house waiting for the workmen to finish. She abhors the noise and she bristles at the time the kids take from her. Not that either of us has quantified the time spent. But when she told me that this wasn't what she had spent $70,000 to buy, I bristled, but knew this was a choice we'd both made.

Moving Your Parents into a Senior Facility

Jenny's parents were determined to stay in their own home until they died. Not an uncommon wish, especially when both partners are alive. Moving and making new friends gets harder as we age. However, her father had chronic emphysema, and her mother's arthritis was rapidly progressing, making caregiving and simple household tasks almost impossible, even with daily help. Apart from the prohibitive cost of 24-hour care, it became clear that soon the house would be too much for them.

> *Women are the most likely seniors to live alone. In 1996, 38 percent of all women aged 65 and older were living on their own, compared with just 12 percent of women aged 45 to 64.*

Having recognized this likelihood some years before her parents, Jenny had started the process of researching nursing homes that would take both her parents in their present state of health and which would provide good and caring facilities when the inevitable degeneration occurred. Once a suitable facility was found, the biggest challenge for Jenny was persuading her parents to make the move while they could still enjoy the self-contained couples unit. Eventually they "caved" and so began the often painful process of paring down the possessions of a lifetime—which for years had found space in a three-bedroom house—to fit in the new tiny one-bedroom apartment.

"My mother, especially, had a terrible time choosing what to take. Because we're a fairly big family, we were able to distribute many possessions within the family, which gave her some comfort. We undertook the task gradually, clearing out one room at a time. It took several weeks. There were still many things left, and we decided to deal with these once my parents were comfortably settled. It would have caused too much distress for them to witness the inevitable garage sale."

If one can persuade parents to tackle the task of paring down before the need to do so becomes urgent, the process can be less hurtful. During the course of clearing out and up, Jenny recalls that the family laughed, cried, and above all, remembered.

IT'S NEVER A CAKEWALK

While it is possible to make all the arrangements for caring for an elderly parent in one great flurry of activity or need, sometimes it is a process fraught with onerous drudgery and guilt. And it can go on and on, risking job and family ties and peace of mind. Paula's story has all these elements and as she remembers all the years of acrimony and bitterness, she acknowledges that part of her character has been burnished in the fire of her mother's spite.

When I was 11, my father left our home, and at school I instantly became one of only two children who came from a "broken home"—always pronounced in rather hushed tones. My "protector" had left and was not exactly persistent in his pursuit of equal visitation. It was 1955, and at some point my mother arbitrarily decided to suspend any visits with my father. So it wasn't until I was 16 and had a vague notion of my rights that I was able to see him again on a regular basis, more at my insistence than his. Our history together was characterized by infrequent communication, but when we did meet we usually had fun—it was his passion for art and art history that touched off a similar spark in me.

Fast forward 21 years, to Canada. My father's death was an unexpected shock. Out of the blue came the call that he had died. Within hours, my daughter and I were in England attending his funeral. The whole experience was shocking, wrenching, and brutal. I was completely distanced from the whole affair as I watched his siblings take over everything—the arrangements, the process. It did not occur to me until much later that I might be my father's only voice in these affairs. It was too late. The burial had been arranged. The tribute was ghastly—I have no idea who briefed the rabbi, but he rendered a depressing statement of my father's life, one that harped on his later loneliness and depression—with no mention of the color and fun of his earlier years. A sad eulogy for a painter.

My time to make this up to my father came eight years later when my cousin and I were invited by a prestigious arts periodical to write a profile of his life and work. I embarked upon an odyssey that would take two years and which put me in touch with people all over the world for whom my father had painted. I didn't know I had that many tears to shed, or so many unasked questions.

He was 70 when he died, and I was 40 when the profile was published. That was in 1984; 18 years have passed and I will always regret that we did not know each other better and that our respect for one another came so much later in our lives. But it did come. During my last visit, I gave him a limited-edition art book, which had taken me two years to produce. I held my breath as he gently removed the book from its slipcase, carefully examining every page, feeling the texture of the paper and the cloth, then putting it down on his lap and saying, "You make beautiful books." Validation.

From my mother, validation was unlikely—no matter what tack I tried or which furrow I plowed. It would be an understatement to say our relationship was dysfunctional. Life with her was riddled with abuse, and I spent far too many years trying to unknot the pretzel I had become in trying to figure out what I had done and how I could get some—any—love. All the knot-tying being liberally sprinkled with resentment, hatred, and guilt.

Armed with this baggage, I would spend more than 10 years trying to supervise the needs of my aging, bitter mother, who lived 4,000 miles away, on her own. I learned a lot. In hindsight, I don't think I've ever questioned my motives as I did each and every decision connected with my mother's care. Suddenly, the impotent child had some power. Was I making a certain decision based on revenge? Did I just want to walk away from the whole responsibility? Why should I even be responsible? Time to grow up and look at this woman, my mother, dispassionately and try to figure out what she wanted.

I think a whole army of caregivers, social workers, benefits agencies, etcetera, tried to figure out what she wanted—it changed daily. Appointments made were constantly broken, vital assessments were continually delayed, bills went unpaid, utilities were disconnected, and at one point the bailiff had to be appeased—all in all, she led a merry dance. If I had been there, we might have been able to organize her care a little better. Would it have made a difference? I don't know; I suspect not. Consequently, my life was in turmoil, I never knew the nature or the time of the next frantic call from London. No planning manual or "How to get your parents to confide in you" seminar was going to help this situation. I realized early on that I would have to play it all by ear.

During this period, I had become a grandmother twice, broken my heart, had a brief chat with cancer, downsized my company, turned 50, and was supporting my daughter as her marriage and her health came apart. There were many balls to be juggled. Without my friends holding me up ...

Good stuff did come out of this experience. With some amazement, I came to see that my mother's caustic tongue and autocratic attitude caused as much pain to others as it had to me. She was immensely stubborn—fueled by prejudice and paranoia—characteristics that made her incredibly vulnerable to those who might take advantage of her isolation. Surprisingly, I found myself protecting her. Constantly, I was called on to make her caregivers aware of the instances of abuse—as relayed by mother, which made communication rather tricky, given her proclivity for exaggeration. I became her guardian, albeit from such a distance. So, after all, there was some sort of perverse validation—it wasn't just me, I had not been singled out for her abusive treatment.

There would be no last-minute reconciliation; it was a hard slog all the way. Mother exacted a heavy toll on herself and others. When I stood by her coffin, which seemed disproportionately small compared to her enormous influence, I was able to wish her peace and rest. An epiphany? Perhaps.

Several years have passed and my daughter, now in her mid-30s, is facing her father's premature death. I watch as she struggles with her emotions toward a man who has been very absent from her life. It's hard to watch, stand back, and just be there when she needs me, as she attempts to make peace in her own way. Perhaps now I know enough to help her recognize the ambiguities, and I know too that only she can come to terms with them. We have come full circle.

AND IN THE END

Nothing, it seems, can ever be enough for a parent who is dying. And it's instructive to understand why. A great deal has been said about guilt. How it plays the neurotic child in us trying to care for our increasingly helpless parents in order to somehow repay them for the years they looked after us. Certainly, part of my job as a physician is to be a cushion against the groundswell of my patients' guilt over their impotence in the face of their parents' infirmity or death. A guilt that left unchecked can diminish all their lives. But while guilt may be fashionable and "safe" to talk about, what I often see is a demonstration of the most extraordinary sacrifices being made for our parents—throwing away our careers, leaving our country, deferring our own needs in order to care for them in their dotage. And I think it is because of that

> *While guilt may be "safer" to talk about, the most extraordinary sacrifices are made for our parents because of that much simpler and more powerful emotion called love.*

much simpler and more powerful emotion called love. We do all this because we love our parents, just as, for the most part, they love us.

So how should you show your increasingly ill parents that you love them? How can you give them the death they deserve? What you can do is enlist your family doctor in helping you search out the full range of help that's available. Not just the "old folks" homes, but the community agencies, church, and "homeland" organizations that are still part of our fraying social safety net. You can go to your local high school and plug in to their volunteer programs that send teenagers into homes to cook for the elderly and read to them.

You can also do your entire family a favor by asking your physician about directives for care, since medical technology now enables an extension of life far beyond what our parents may want. For instance, establishing a durable power of attorney for health care, which must be properly witnessed and in most provinces requires a lawyer to execute the document. At the very least, a discussion about creating a living will examine the question of what our parents wish to have done at the end of their days. Still, when all is said and done, we continue to spend more than 80 percent of all health care dollars on the first year and the last year of life. It is their death, just as some day it will be ours, and we should be able to control it, embrace it, and own it as much as we can.

10

Why the Next 40 Can Be Better Than the First 50

We shall not cease from exploration
And the end of all our exploring
Will be to arrive where we started
And know the place for the first time.

T.S. Eliot, *Four Quartets*

By the time we reach our 50s, we have been shaped by significant events, forged by innumerable emotions and, are, we hope, at a place where the peace of acceptance and wisdom rather than the fear of aging has settled somewhere in our souls. Since we live in a culture that is perpetually bombarding us with messages that tell us to fight the signs of aging, our wisdom is precious and hard won.

Many provisos surround this chapter's title: providing you have good health, providing you have the material resources—these are just two. Even if these are limited by constraints beyond our control, the inescapable truth is that the longer we stay on the road, the more we lose: faculties, friends, and partners. How will we cope and with what will we replace that which we lose? To what do we look forward and will our spirit be our mainstay?

I am constantly amazed and inspired at the will and strength of the women in my practice as they ponder these questions and seek the answers with courage and adaptability. Each will take a different route and come to terms with aging in her own indomitable fashion. My belief is that the first 50 years provide the glue in the structure that is our lives, which in turn becomes the platform upon which we stand to view the next 40, or for that matter 50, years. The higher the platform, the farther we see. The stronger the platform, the more we can bear and remain standing. As I have gone through this book, it becomes clear that there are some obvious messages that surface from caring for patients and from the long experience in living our lives together.

I have been present at many birthings and had the rare experience of witnessing the wonder of new life and new family configurations. I have watched young children nurtured in these families and been struck by how early the evolution of temperament and character becomes evident. I watch mothers mother and become elastic in how they adapt to the needs and demands of their dependent treasures. I watch the struggles as children grow, first in school, then as they enter the mainstream. There are sometimes pitched battles with authority of any kind, be it parental or societal. There is much anxiety generated by our penchant for diagnosis—oppositional behavior disorder, anorexia or bulimia, depression, attention deficit disorder. We spend millions getting the kids through school systems that seem not so much institutions of learning but obstructions in the path of acquiring tools for living.

Whatever the hurdles, I am always stuck by the simple fact of how well our kids turn out. I believe this result all comes from that essential moment in the delivery suite where it all begins and everything is possible in those tears of love and thankfulness. The great gift for those babies who are now teens or perhaps by now young adults having their own offspring is that they are a source of pride and joy for us all. Now we can bask in their accomplishments and only wonder at the difficult years, thankful that they are past. Which brings us to being grandparents.

This is the reward for all the worry and effort that underlie the rearing years, of this I am sure. I see it in my midlife patients as much as in our friends. In the birthing unit, I watch as grandparents attend, rejoice, and thank their children for that precious gift. I encourage the presence of mothers in the delivery suite, so many have had such memories of their own truncated or out-of-control birthing experiences. Grandchildren have a wondrous effect in shifting the time sense and altering priorities for otherwise very busy women. Learning begins anew and becomes, a far as I can tell, a wholly different show. Now there is time to focus on how the world looks to a small child and share that view. There is less drive to acquire prescribed information and more interest in exploration. There are gifts of memory and storytelling.

I have watched families fracture and women gather their strength and resolve to go forward. The same resolve shines through around other hurdles: job loss, illness, loneliness, the burden of elder care, aging itself.

Even in seemingly small areas, I see the shifts of adaptability. Five years ago, I know the Internet was not an essential tool for midlife women. However, in writing the chapter on breast cancer, it became patently clear that accessing information on the Net is the only way for affected women

> *The Internet is also the access road for support and advocacy and from there, to activism.*

and their family members to keep abreast of the trials and treatments. It is also the access road for support and advocacy and from there, I believe, to activism. If a 90-year-old woman can take herself off to a computer course in order to learn more than how to turn her computer on to get e-mails from grandchildren and great-grandchildren around the world, can we in our middle years do less?

Many of the same pathways of adaptability emerge from writing about heart disease, bones, memory. I consider that most of my days are spent talking to women about changing their lives in order to be able to do physical work. What a surprise, since most of us feel we have spent years on a mental treadmill. We are tired all the time and equally burdened by a terrible sense of tension and the pressure of no time. No time to look out for our own needs let alone really address those of our children, parents, or friends. I noted in the first chapter that the time pressure falls dramatically after 55. All to the good, I say, and I use this as a beacon for my time-weary women.

Recently, I wrote an article that promoted marathon running as an appropriate goal for midlife woman. My belief, which applies as much to me as to my readers, is that women are inherently already trained to undertake this kind of activity. They have endurance, stamina, doggedness, and discipline. And the bonus while doing it is time alone as they undertake the long training runs. Imagine the luxury of three hours alone with your thoughts or your tapes and no phone. And it's guilt free. Even teenage children stand down when mom is out on a run—ducking in case she should ask if they want to come along. We are talking months of alone-time here—it takes one hundredth of the energy to run a marathon as it does to train for one.

Five years ago there were few middle-aged women in the two big People's Marathons in New York City and Washington, DC. This year in Washington alone, 1,000 of the 15,000 runners were middle-aged women. Lastly, in my shilling for this as an option, I would suggest that in the middle years there may be a hiatus, however brief, between getting the children away and seeing the caring of parents approach, which provides a small opportunity of time to undertake the endeavor.

Physical capacity doesn't apply just to things like running. As we have seen, such activities lend themselves to building endurance and cardiovascular reserve. But we need flexibility and strength in equal measure for the span of life. Dance and yoga lend themselves admirably for this purpose for many of my patients. Establishing a routine is not so arduous that it cannot be undertaken with more than grudging effort. Women, as we have come to appreciate, respond to a social context for exercise as much as they do for quilting bees or reading groups.

As for relationships and the changing configurations of roles that women play, redefining them through the years, once again we gain from the inherent strength in our platform. Long ago, during the course of looking after my patients, it occurred to me that women do not change their essential selves, even though they may change the semblance of who they look like or what they do as their life's work. This becomes even more obvious when you look at the roles they undertake in the "mature years," when there is no or perhaps less requirement to secure a living. The phrase "to give back" has always had a certain blandness of spirit if not intent, as though

> *Women do not change their essential selves, even though they may change the semblance of who they look like or what they do as their life's work.*

there may be a prescription that would repay some sort of obligation to society at large. However, the phrase does not begin to reflect the passion that I see in women who suddenly find themselves galvanized into action for a cause or a purpose.

The ways in which they choose to take action are as numerous and varied as the women themselves. Some will take on the care of a grandchild or teach or work in a local senior's home; others discover the latent activist in their souls and decide to lobby, whether it be for that long sought-after crossing guard by the local school or to found an organization like Mothers Against Drunk Driving (MADD). Whatever the size or scope of the task, it is at this point that all the experiences and all the learning and skill sets acquired during the first 50 years come together—a perfect fusion with which to go forward for the next 40.

I now want to recount the stories of three women who changed the source of their livelihood and fulfillment. Each of these women had served long and at times happily in the kind of careers women are so good at—one was a teacher; one, a volunteer; and one, a social activist. Given a perfect world, they may have kept on teaching, volunteering, and activating for the rest of their lives. But it's not a perfect static world and circumstances have led each of these women to exercise all their skill sets and morph seamlessly from one occupation to another. In an interesting role reversal, each of these three women became what one of the others had been.

These women, like myself, had heard that our children will inherit a workplace where having five or six careers will be the norm rather than the exception. These kinds of prophecies land softly on us, I suppose, because we know that in our 50s, we are somewhat immune to the wrenching and new skill-building needed to change from a 56-year-old middle manager to a 57-year-old entrepreneur.

An Educator Turned Counsellor

She had retired with full accolades after a life in teaching and educational consulting. Why go into a war-torn country to do something that was unfamiliar and perhaps dangerous and which for sure would have hardship embedded within its very fiber? Why? Never an easy question for most of the patients I ask, since the answer always seems too trite or too amorphous. Perhaps it's also because by the time you are asking the question, the reasons are no longer important or the experience overrides whatever has driven the decision in the first place.

This was certainly the case for my patient. She was asked; she went. And she has been back twice because she was able to help. Her presence was her unique contribution in the effort to seek out the village women in the ravaged towns and help them rebuild their own support nets. The rescuers assembled in bombed-out barns and houses and invited the villagers—almost all women and children—to come and talk about their misery and hardship and seek solace. More tangibly, the intent was also to provide a means of providing relief to restart living. But the grannies, the ancient ones, would not come. They could not see anything there for them until they saw the gray-haired one.

"I wasn't very good at this work. The coordinator who was a social worker was excellent in the groups and they really were helpful, but because I was there, they could get the older women to come as well. There was some comfort for them in seeing me. After I returned home, I knew I would go back, and so I arranged things a little better for myself in order to stay in touch with my own children, who are all over the world, and with my companion at home. It is very lonely when you are out there without communication."

Clearly, it was not only the gray hair that made her presence so effective. She oozes calmness, her voice is a lilt, she looks at you straight on with intent and warmth, and you know there is kindness present. She moves with assurance. She exudes strength and knowledge and capacity. She is sensible and sure. All the grannies divined this in a flash, and that was their comfort. All her students through the years had divined the same qualities, and that was their blessing.

AN ACTIVIST TURNED EDUCATOR

Judy Rebick is a long-time patient whose name is a household word. Over the years she has reinvented herself in many modes, so the latest, as an educator, should come as no surprise. But it is part of her life's pathway that has thrown this inadvertently in her way, and with characteristic zeal she has risen to the challenge. " I said I would never do this again and here I am doing it," she says.

"This," of course, defines both the woman and her life, which is to say, holding down two full-time jobs. Crisscrossing the country on speaking tours has become the

> *I myself have never been able to find out precisely what feminism is: I only know that people call me a feminist whenever I express sentiments that differentiate me from a doormat or a prostitute.*
>
> *—Rebecca West*

basis of huge networks for information-sharing in the conduct of her second job—political activism, or community work as she broadly defines it.

"I'm too old for this," she says, coughing with a dry irritating little rattle. "I've had this cough for two weeks and can't get rid of it." There is no milk for the coffee; the dailies, strewn over the kitchen table, have already been read for content; and there is a flurry of chat on the cellular phone as meetings and responses are planned.

We settle in. When Judy was 10, her parents and two brothers came from the rich Jewish life of Brooklyn to a stark suburbia in north Toronto. She always felt different, always felt she had to fight for her rights. In many ways she attributes the patterning of her life as her response to a domineering and abusive father, whom she had to defy in order to survive. As a young girl, part of that survival was to write stories, which she has done ever since, honing her skills over the years. If her backbone arose out of the fractious relationship with her father, her verve stems from her mother, whom she describes as a true feminist. There was no differentiation in the expectations of Judy and her two brothers. In fact, Judy admits, since she was more manipulative, she managed to do less domestic work than her brothers.

Her mother's true liberation came at age 89 with the death of her husband. Now at 91, she is out every day to play bridge at the senior's club. The children introduced her to an Internet site so she could upgrade her bridge skills, but she took herself to a computer class to learn about computing. Now she has found the game-show channel and is in seventh heaven.

The other part of Judy's survival/salvation came when she was an undergraduate at McGill University, where, as a writer on the university newspaper in the mid-1960s era of youth and radical thinking, she found others who too felt they were misfits. Her politicization grew out of those connections. She became bilingual by living with a fellow Trotskyite who spoke only French, and learnt French well enough to do simultaneous translation.

Her political activism matured as she did, and by the 1980s her name became synonymous with the Ontario Coalition for Abortion Services and Henry Morgentaler, and the National Action Committee and feminism. She became the public spokesperson for the abortion rights movement and was good at it. Television required a different style of presentation and for that she went to the TV clips of none other than Ronald Reagan, in her opinion the most effective TV presence in terms of emotional appeal and impact. Reporters were also on hand to help her through the rough spots. "They would take me out back and suggest a different line for the next time," she chortles.

She was and remains the master of the sound byte, but it was not until she saved Dr. Morgantaler from an attack by an assailant armed with shears that the media began to focus on this brassy, outspoken woman. At that point, her other attributed sound bytes became her own. As she moved into the visual media with her TV talk shows, helpful suggestions came from the technicians and support staff. There was grooming and makeup and a clothing allowance.

During this period of recognition and new beginnings, her nephew came to live with her full-time. With little planning, she found them an apartment that was big enough. "But I had never had a dependant and the second week in, I went to Montreal, leaving home without money or food," she recalls. A troubled youth who had been hospitalized for a period, Judy's nephew was on the edge and without a shred of self-confidence. Judy's singular decision in dealing with his behavior during a period of four months was to never criticize him directly—not easy since he was bent on testing limits, like coming in at 4 o'clock in the morning. Well, that wasn't

> *Red plush tops and net stockings—wow! Where did he get them? The approach worked. Within three weeks he stopped dressing so bizarrely and staying out all night.*

going to work for Judy, since it woke her up and she needed her sleep, but his time constraints were otherwise his own business. Going out in red plush tops and net stockings—wow! Where did he get them? The approach worked. Within three weeks he stopped dressing so bizarrely and staying out all night.

He loved to cook, and Judy would arrive home from her show at 9 o'clock to find dinner waiting. No one had ever done that for her before. Gradually, he settled into school, and this year he will graduate from university on the dean's honor list as the best student it's had in 20 years. "He's a beautiful kid and he wants to be a writer and he's a good writer. It was the best decision I ever made, to be able to give back in this way, and it was very healing for me," Judy says. During that time and since, I have come to see a different Judy, warm in nurturing, and mellow in companionship.

Another relative, a niece, moved in with them. Now Judy needed a three-bedroom apartment. "I've lived with kids for six years and I much more enjoy living with them than alone." This may seem odd, until you appreciate how she makes all her decisions. It was as her nephew prepared to move on that she bought her house and settled in. All her decisions are made on the spot, if it "feels right."

That peculiar Rebick methodology also propelled her latest venture into the Internet-based Rabble.ca. While she was doing her CBC online column, speaking out against the bombing in Kosovo, she received a phenomenal 200 to 300 e-mail responses per column. "Never happened before. I thought, What is this about? I mean, never did I receive that kind of response from the columns I wrote or the TV shows. They were thoughtful, interesting letters from all over the world and the people who wrote them didn't know me other than as a writer for the CBC. But I thought, this is really something."

That led to many discussions across the land with journalists, media people, and activists about what a national online newspaper might look like. It was from there that young people were identified as the most likely users of the service. But there needed to be some provisos. "Kids don't give a damn about my opinion on the war on terrorism. It's about their opinion, and they want a venue for debate and discussion. You can't do that without a good moderator. So as part of Rabble.ca there are three components: News and Views, Content Co-op, and Babble, an interactive chat site. And it's a real community. We have 1,700 registered users. I think it's hard for us at our age to understand it because it moves so fast. The day after September 11, a kid in Sault Ste. Marie went to the library and took out the Koran. He has been quoting passages on the online discussions about Islam. He is a genius and he's 15. Imagine that connectivity." Judy's own e-mail address is on the Rabble site.

As to what is in the future for today's young women? Again, it's not their feminist image that is lacking. "A whole generation of women have grown up believing in their own equality and that's incredibly powerful," Judy says. She may wonder where the independent women's movement is going but understands that movements by their very nature change. Rather, she worries about the relationship between men and women. Allowing that there is also a whole segment of young men out there that are not domineering and treat women with respect, she feels there is still a core of sexist men that women still are attracted to and abused by. But the real issue—out of her mouth before the question is out of mine—is body image. "I don't understand it and it bothers me because I think it is an epidemic and it's a hideous attitude about food. It's today's guilty pleasure-eating, or eating as sin. My niece's friends in the last two years have dropped 10 pounds and they think it's beautiful, but it's not."

What does she worry about for herself? Not what's in the future, that's for sure: "I try not to think about it, though my brother and his wife and I talk about living together at some point. I never put a cent away for retirement until I was 45. Given what I'm doing now, back in community work, I'll never be a high-income earner. And you never want to rely on kids anyway, but I know I'm the third parent for my nephew and my two nieces and I know they will help me out if it comes to that. I hope to keep writing books because you can do that until you are pretty old, and I loved the process of writing my book, though I couldn't do it full-time—it would drive me nuts."

"Look to your mother," I respond. "The way looks clear."

A VOLUNTEER TURNED CONSULTANT

She was already past 60 and had worked for the government just long enough for her coworkers to realize the need for a retirement party. She had come to this, her third career, later than most, since she had not even begun her first until she was turning 50. That was when she decided her children were old enough to understand her taking leave of their alcoholic father. She needed work not only to support herself and the children but also to redefine herself. She didn't quite know what she was at that point, but as she launched herself in Al-Anon and 12-step work, she began to emerge from passivity and somnolence. A friend gave her a break and she joined his travel company, taking groups to Europe and any number of exotic locations, honing newfound people skills. Other talents emerged.

Utilizing her long-buried facility with school and community fund-raising and people skills, she began to offer her services to organizations requiring terminal doggedness and endless good cheer. Two lucrative government contracts later, she applied for and got her first serious job. She was past 50 and wanted the stable income and benefits and perks that a bureaucratic job had to offer. There was rigidity to contend with, but she managed to flow within its constraints, traveling widely now that the children were well launched. She worked within smaller communities, helping them develop their strategies, and it was the kind of up-close and personal work that suited her nature.

Her plans for travel and her spirited nature led her into language classes and dance lessons. So to her retirement party, her staff brought the Latin dance instructor of the classes she had been going to, and he and she put on a show. Then it was off to Europe for an extended tour on her own time and in her own fashion. Now she has returned and her new venue is yet to be determined. But one truth is evident: her children are the anchors, she is the firefly.

For me, as I approach 60, I remain touched at what a breathtaking world we have and by the wonderful women I look after. This is a book of hope for all of us as we breach the 50-year mark and look ahead. Here is the story of how I met that rare landmark.

When did I know it was over? When he didn't take the dog away for the weekend trip. As surely as sunset, I knew this chapter was closed. It wasn't that I represented the dog. It wasn't that I would now be saddled with walking, caring, feeding, patting the underfoot dog, and the kids for that matter. No, somehow it was a symbolic gesture of family leave-taking—finished, no more playing at the roles, no more playing out tired routines. In a way, the dog had been holding the thin fabric of this frail marriage together in the same way each of our children had done in turn and in their own subterranean ways. I had always been suspicious that the dramatic gesture, and the flights from school, and the terrible morning stomach pains were symbols in their own right. But it took the dog.

True, the thought of leaving had flitted through my mind, but it had flitted right on out as I continued to hide out in the hospital's delivery suite. When my mother eloped with my father-in-law, it had crossed

> *Backed into freedom was how I came to view my newfound state, and it awakened long-submerged desires and states. For one, I began to really like men again. For another, I scrapped with my kids—loud, wild harangues.*

my mind that I was trapped in my own relationship. "I'll never get out," I thought, but I was soldiering on and hiding and not too reflective of my thoughts as I "made the party" for the 69- and 71-year-old elopees.

Backed into freedom was how I came to view my newfound state, and it awakened long-submerged desires and states. For one, I began to really like men again. Not just a wildly reconnected libido but a pleasure in being around them that I hadn't realized I had lost. I got in shape, tuned my body, and found a long-buried pride in being strong and having endurance. For another, I scrapped with my kids—loud, wild harangues—testing the edge, it seemed, for us who fit more the model of quiet, desperate types.

Was I starting over? More like staying on top of myself. I was free to a point. But over the next year I would let go of a number of childhood myths, like your job as a parent is to provide a house for your children. The house was bleeding me and so it had to go. Debt had dogged me all my life, and we had lived far beyond our means. Sell it all, downsize your peripherals, get out of debt. Once clear of that, with a more modest rental, I suddenly could see my dream: a walk in history on the Appalachian Trail. It took a year to plan, prepare the children, arrange a locum for my practice. There was never any question about not going once it was conceived and it happened.

I was 50.

The "other" in my life at that point was Bob. We came together almost by happenstance, and the match-up seemed draped with fatal flaws from the outset. I, full of raging hormones and only wanting to use men at that point, he out of treatment for addiction and declaring bankruptcy. How did this stand a chance? My children didn't think it did, and they said so loudly. And anyway, I wasn't sure that I had ever really been capable of giving over my heart to a man. Our dry run played out on the Appalachian Trail. Through 900 miles and much sweat, we arrived in the end at a different place and went the next step and then the next.

It has been 10 years and many hikes. But when did I give my heart? Not in the formality of our marriage ceremony, though it was a lovely thing and we wanted our friends to know our commitment to one another. "Backed into loving" still seems to be my modus operandi. We had gone backpacking deep into the Rockies, deeper, farther, longer than ever before. It had rained hard through the night and in the morning we had packed the sodden tents and climbed high. We reached the top of the Continental Divide and there, watching my man—short guy, red hair—standing 20 feet below, a human flagpole tethering a bright yellow tent-fly flapping in the breeze at 6,000 feet, I sat on the mountaintop and wept.

So here is my wish for us all. That there is still magic ahead, waiting to enchant us, be it worldly or with children; that we can remain physically strong and spiritually whole; that we are able to acknowledge the wisdom of our years as the years of wisdom evolve. And if not peace, then at the very least, that we have peace of mind in the love we have to give and the love we receive.

ENDNOTES

Chapter 2

1. Eisenberg, D.M. et al. "Trends in Alternative Medicine Use in the United States, 1990–1997: Results of a Follow-up National Survey," *JAMA* 1998; 280: 1569–1575.

2. Sherwin, B.B. "Estrogen and or Androgen Replacement and Cognitive Functioning in Surgically Menopausal Women," *Psychoneuroendocrin* 1988; 10: 325–351.

Chapter 3

1. Powell, K.E. et al. "Physical Activity and the Incidence of Coronary Heart Disease," *Ann Rev Public Health* 1987; 8: 253–287.

2. Pate, R. et al. "Physical Activity and Public Health: A Recommendation from the Centers of Disease Control and Prevention and the American College of Sports Medicine," *JAMA* 1995; 273: 402–407.

3. Lee, I.M. et al. "Exercise Intensity and Longevity in Men: The Harvard Alumni Health Study," *JAMA* 1995; 273: 1179–1184.

4. Blair, S.N. et al. "Physical Fitness and All Cause Mortality: A Prospective Study of Healthy Men and Women," *JAMA* 1989; 262: 2395–2401.

5. Balady, G.J. "Cardiac Rehab Programs," *Circulation* 1994; 90: 1602–1610.

6. Kavanagh, T. "Can Women Benefit from Exercise Cardiac Rehabilitation Advances in Cardio-Pulmonary Rehabilitation?" *Human Kinetics* 2000; 78–88.

7. Burr, M.L. et al. "Effects of Changes in Fat Fish Fibre Intakes on Death and Myocardial Reinfarction Trial DART," *Lancet* 1989; 2(866): 757–761.

8. Shepherd, J. et al. "Prevention of Coronary Heart Disease with Pravastatin in Men with Hypercholesteremia," *NEJM* 1995; 333: 1301–1307.

9. Leaf, A. "Final Report of the Lyon Diet Heart Study," *Circulation* 1999; 99(6): 733–735.

10. 4-S Group. "Randomized Trial of Cholesterol Lowering in 4444 Patients with Coronary Artery Disease: The Scandinavian Simvastatin Survival Study," Lancet 1994; 344: 1383-1389.

11. Sheperd, J. et al. "West of Scotland Coronary Prevention Study: Identification of High Risk Groups and Comparison with Other Coronary Intervention Trials," *Lancet* 1996; 348: 1339–1342.

Chapter 4

1. Rubin, S.M. et al. "Hormone Therapy to Prevent Disease and Prolong Life in Postmenopausal Women," *Ann Internal Medicine* 1992; 117(12): 1016–1037.

Chapter 5

1. Gail, M.H. et al. "Projecting Individualized Probabilities of Developing Breast Cancer for White Females Who Are Being Examined Annually," *J Natl Cancer Inst* 1989; 81: 1879–1886.

2. Chaudhry, R. et al. "Breast Cancer Survival by Teaching Status of the Initial Treating Hospital," *CMAJ* 2001; 164(2): 183–188.

Chapter 6

1. *Canadian Study of Health and Aging*, 1991. A study funded by the Seniors' Independence Research Program, administered by the National Health Research Development Program, and coordinated by the University of Ottawa and the Division of Aging and Seniors, Health Canada.

2. Groneck, S. et al. *Human Aging 11*. US Public Service Monograph, Washington, DC, 1971.

Chapter 9

1. Canada, Minister of National Health and Welfare. *Ageing and Independence: Overview of a National Survey*. Ottawa: Supply and Services Canada, 1993.

RECOMMENDED RESOURCES

In researching information on the Internet, bear in mind the caveat "consider the source." The following sites give reliable information on specific subjects. In addition, almost all the universities both here and overseas are dependable sources.

In Canada, the Canadian Health Network site (**www.canadian-health-network.ca**) is constantly being updated and augmented; as well it provides links to other helpful sites.

Many of the hospitals have good websites. For example, Women's College Hospital (**www.sunnybrookandwomens.on.ca**) publishes a monthly newsletter entitled *Women's Health Matters*, highlights of which are published on its website, **www.womenshealthmatters.ca**.

Chapter 2

www.afriendindeed.ca
A Friend Indeed is a respected source of understandable and reliable information about the menopausal transition, independent of any vested interests.

www.tnp.com/encyclopedia
The Natural Pharmacists' Encyclopedia is a good site to gather basic information on herbs, alternative therapies, and drug interactions.

www.pitt.edu/~cbw/altm.html
University of Pittsburg's alternative medicine site.

www.quackwatch.com
Quackwatch, Inc., was founded by Dr. Stephen Barrett in 1969 and is a non-profit corporation whose purpose is to combat health-related frauds, myths, fads, and fallacies.

Chapter 3

www.canadian-health-network.ca
The network is a partnership between nongovernmental organizations and Health Canada.

www.heartandstroke.ca
Heart and Stroke Foundation of Canada

www-hsl.mcmaster.ca/tomflem/breastcancer.html
One of the most comprehensive Canadian websites for breast cancer information for patients, families, and caregivers.

www.framingham.com/heart/index.htm
This site documents past findings of the Framingham Heart Study and emerging risk factors.

Chapter 4

www.canadian-health-network.ca
The network is a partnership between nongovernmental organizations and Health Canada.

www.osteoporosis.ca
Osteoporosis Society of Canada.

Chapter 5

If you type the keywords "breast cancer" into the Google search engine, it will find 1,260,000 sites. You can reduce that number by adding the words "Canadian" (23,400 sites found) or "advocacy" (35,400 sites found). Here are some excellent sites that will lead to a number of subject areas, from clinical trials to support groups and advocacy.

www.cancer.ca
Canadian Cancer Society.

www.nlm.nih.gov/medlineplus
Medline Plus Health Information is a service of the National Library of Medicine.

www.cbcn.ca
The Canadian breast cancer network is a national network and voice of breast cancer survivors.

www.hc.sc.gc.ca/hpb
The Government of Canada's Cancer Bureau.

www.wellspring.ca
Wellspring is a support center for people with cancer and their loved ones.

Chapter 6

www.canadian-health-network.ca
The network is a partnership between nongovernmental organizations and Health Canada.

www.alzheimers.ca
The Alzheimer Society of Canada provides many resources on its website and a quarterly publication, *Alzheimer's Care Quarterly*.

www.howtocare.com
How to Care, Inc., is the result of Karen Henderson's 14-year caregiving odyssey with her father. The site provides useful data and an opportunity to discuss and share information with other caregivers.

Chapter 7

www.caseyfamilyservices.org
Casey Family Services assists vulnerable children and families.

www.earlscourt.on.ca
The mandate of Earlscourt Child and Family Centre is putting children "back together" by keeping kids in school and out of trouble through family-focused children's mental health services for children with aggressive and delinquent behaviors.

www.parentsforyouth.com
Parents for Youth is dedicated to helping parents of conduct-disordered youths.

www.toughlove.org
TOUGHLOVE International is a nonprofit, self-help organization that provides ongoing education and active support to families.

Books

How to talk so Kids will Listen; How to Listen so Kids will Talk, by Adele Faber and Elaine Mazlish, Avon Books, 1999.

Kids Are Worth It, by Barbara Colorosa, Penguin Books of Canada, 2001.

Real Gorgeous: The Truth About Body and Beauty, by Kaz Cooke, W.W. Norton, 1996.

When Girls Feel Fat: Helping Girls Through Adolescence, by Sandra Friedman, HarperCollins 1997.

Chapter 9

www.howtocare.com
How to Care, Inc., is the result of Karen Henderson's 14-year caregiving odyssey with her father. The site provides useful data and an opportunity to discuss and share information with other caregivers.

www.cihi.ca (link to seniors)
Canadian Institute for Health Information.

www.seniors.gc.ca
Government of Canada's senior's online site.

www.50plus.com
The Canadian Association for Retired People (CARP) site supplies useful links and information through its electronic magazine.

www.hc-sc.gc.ca/seniors-aines
The National Advisory Council on Aging site also publishes a quarterly newsletter called *Expression*.

www.rgp.toronto.on.ca/iddg/eol.htm
University of Toronto and University of Ottawa collaborated to produce *A Guide to End of Life Care for Seniors*, which can be downloaded from the website.

www.rgp.toronto.on.ca
For application for outreach assessment, write to:
Regional Geriatric Program
Contact: Dr. Rory Fisher
Sunnybrook Women's Health Sciences Centre
2075 Bayview Avenue, H478
Toronto, ON M4N 3M5
Tel: 416-480-6802

INDEX